BACKING U!
Lite

A Quick-Read Guide to
BACKING YOUR PASSION
and Achieving Career Success

VAUGHAN EVANS

Published by Business & Careers Press
PO Box 59814
2 Mortlake High Street
London SW14 8UR
www.businessandcareerspress.com

Printed and bound in the United States of America

First printing 2009

ISBN 978-0-9561391-1-5

**ATTENTION CORPORATIONS, UNIVERSITIES, COLLEG-
ES, AND PROFESSIONAL ORGANIZATIONS:** Quantity
discounts are available on bulk purchases of this book for
educational, professional, or gift purposes, or as premiums
for increasing magazine subscriptions or renewals. Special
books or book excerpts can also be created to fit specific
needs. For information, please contact the publisher.

For Mon

Table of Contents

Part III: BACKING THE *HWYL*

Preface: On Tough Times

This book is primarily addressed to people who are uncertain whether they are in the right job or business. It can help them improve their prospects where they are, or switch to a job or business where their passion lies.

But the techniques apply as effectively to those who are without a job.

The recession of 2008–09 has been the worst for decades. Hundreds of thousands of people have been laid off? Are you one of them?

If so, you should still follow the approach of this book as set out. But with a twist. You'll need to use the past tense to start with. When you were employed, or running your own business, how backable were you? Were subsequent events predictable, or just bad luck? Were they the result of market demand decline, affecting the many, or your relative lack of competitiveness, affecting just you? Part I helps answer those questions.

If you were backable then, and your current circumstances merely unfortunate, what should you be doing now to make yourself more backable for the upturn? Part II can help here.

Suppose, however, that you find you weren't backable in your former job. Your peers may have fared alright through this recession.

This may be the moment to start afresh, to launch into a new career. You may even have a decent severance check to hand, poised for investment in your future. This is your chance to back your passion. Part III is for you.

You won't be the first. Many have faced such a cloud before and found a silver lining. An architect friend was laid off during the great construction recession of 1989–92. She retrained as an osteopath and hasn't looked back since. She turned anxiety at job loss into an opportunity to reshape her life. You could do likewise.

Best of luck!

Introduction

One-half of U.S. employees are dissatisfied with their jobs, up from two-fifths 10 years ago. Likewise, on the other side of the pond, one-half of U.K. employees feel they are "stuck in the wrong job."

Are you one of them?

But are you really in the wrong job or business? Or is it just a case of the grass being greener on the other side of the fence? Are you dissatisfied or unfulfilled for little or no reason? How can you tell?

If you are seriously dissatisfied, it's going to affect your attitude. And that may show up in your performance.

Are you at risk of losing out to others who are more satisfied with what they do?

How do you change to a career where you can be truly satisfied and inspired? To a career in which you can excel?

If you're among the half of employees who *are* satisfied with their jobs, would you like to move to an even better job? Within your company or organization? Or to a new one? How can you improve your chances of suc-

Note: The employee satisfaction surveys above were conducted by The Conference Board, February 2007 (for the US), and Cranfield School of Management, March 2005 (for the UK).

cess? Would you like to do what you're doing now—but as a self-employed businessperson?

Backing U! LITE helps you answer these questions. Imagine you were an investor. Would *you* back *U* in your current job or business? Is your attitude backable? Are your income prospects that reliable, that promising, over the next few years? Would you be more backable if you worked elsewhere? Perhaps in work to which you felt passionately committed?

Backing U! LITE is set out in three parts:

- *Would You Back U?*—Are you in the right job or business?
- *Becoming More Backable*—If yes, how can you do better in your current job or business?
- *Backing the* Hwyl—If no, how can you switch to a field that inspires you, where the Celtic *hwyl* lies—the spirit, passion, fervor that can lift you to extremes of success?

Before we launch into Part I, let's pause to meet the main cast of characters—see the four shaded boxes. We'll dip into their lives and work challenges throughout this book, whenever we need to translate theoretical advice into everyday reality.

Two of these exemplars, Debi and Selina, are employees, while Cheryl and Roger are self-employed. All of them are in need of backing. We'll find that each of the four will receive backing conditional upon either developing their career where they are now, or switching to another career:

- One employee will contentedly stay put but with some retraining and refocusing (Debi).
- The other employee will shift to self-employment, where her passion lies (Selina).
- One of the self-employed will enthusiastically stay put, and seek to grow and diversify her business (Cheryl).
- The other self-employed person will seek a return to employee status and greater job security (Roger).

These four exemplars won't cover every situation pertinent to every reader, but there should be aspects of at least one of their situations that should prove relevant and illuminating to most.

We'll meet Cheryl and Debi regularly in Parts I and II, but we won't hear of Roger and Selina again until Part III.

Cheryl the Coach

Cheryl is a self-employed tennis coach who has just turned 30. She's contentedly single and lives in the Knob Hill area of Colorado Springs. She's also a keen and talented soccer player and enjoys coaching a local girls' soccer team. She keeps herself in good shape, as she has to, and pursues an active, outdoor lifestyle that is the envy of many of her girlfriends. In the last year or so, she has been thinking about a possible gap in the market whereby she could extend her one-person business and become an employer of up to 10 soccer coaches for one morning and one evening a week. The opportunity excites her.

Debi the Receptionist

Debi is employed as a receptionist at a publishing firm, Little, Stamp & Co, in New York City. She's in her late thirties, married with two boys, aged 8 and 10, who are looked after by a full-time nanny. Debi has the kind of outgoing, bubbly personality that makes her the perfect receptionist. Clients emerge from the elevator after an often miserable journey in the subway or stuck in traffic and find a huge smile and some warm, wisecracking words of welcome. Debi also helps out Little, Stamp when needed at their hospitality events. Recently a marketing assistant was away on maternity leave and Debi helped out with the planning and preparation of a couple of marketing events. She thoroughly enjoyed this work.

Roger the IT Consultant

Roger is a self-employed IT consultant in his late forties. He's married with two daughters aged 16 and 15 and a son of 9, and he works from his home in Kitsilano, a green and spacious suburb of Vancouver, Canada. Roger got laid off from a global software house at the bursting of the dot com bubble in 2001 and has since combined periods of subcontracting with a local Mr. PC Fixit business. He worries over meeting his mortgage commitments and would dearly love a more stable job, as long as it still pays his bills. He has recently read of a scheme to train experienced IT personnel into elementary school IT teachers. It wasn't something he'd ever thought of before, partly because the opportunity hadn't arisen, but he quite liked the idea. He's a member of the Parents Advisory Council at his son's elementary school, so has a fair idea of what the job entails. And he's been a good, highly committed dad, loving nothing more than playing with his kids and their friends. But would he make a good teacher?

Selina the Departmental Manager

Selina is in her late twenties and is the manager of the children's department at Thomas Ellis & Co, a family-owned, rather quaint, 1950s-style fashion and drapery store. It's situated on the Main Street of Stratford-upon-Avon, a market town in the heart of England, 100 miles northwest of London and the birthplace of William Shakespeare 444 years ago. She left Stratford High School at 16 and went straight to work as a sales assistant at another clothes store in the town, where she did well for five years, before being poached and promoted by Ellis's. Marriage and three children soon followed, but Selina was back at work soon after the birth of each child, with her mother looking after the children during working hours.

Further promotion to fashion buyer seems many years distant, and Selina has been pondering an enticing offer from Megastore in London to join as one of six managers reporting to the general manager. She's tempted, but her husband isn't keen on relocating. His administrative job with the local government doesn't pay well, but it's flexible and enables him to take time off when required to look after his elderly and infirm parents. Selina feels stuck. If she has to stay in Stratford, she wonders if she could somehow grasp the opportunity to do what she'd really love to do in life: open her own children's clothing boutique.

Take Care!

The case studies developed for this book are for illustrative purposes only. Readers interested in pursuing one of the careers illustrated, such as sports coaching, reception and marketing services, IT consulting, secondary school teaching, and children's clothing retailing, should conduct their own due diligence on the market following the tools laid out in Part I.

PART I
Would You Back U?

Introduction

You never achieve real success unless you like what you are doing.—Dale Carnegie

In the introduction to this book, we raised the concept of you as an investor considering backing U as a business. Irrespective of whether you're an employee or a self-employed businessperson, would *you* back *U*?

What should you look for when considering whether to back a business? What would a serious pro investor look for, someone who does just this day in, day out. Let's meet one. His name is Chuck Cash.

Sure, Chuck will consider backing U. But he'll also be looking at investing in a host of other business opportunities, including the cast of characters we met in the introduction to this book—Cheryl, Debi, Selina, and Roger. He's going to invest his money where he sees the highest return for the lowest risk. Period.

Don't be fooled by Chuck's name. He doesn't chuck cash any old where. Like other investors, Chuck's choosy where he invests his money. Before he signs a check, he undertakes some serious digging around. If Chuck backed entrepreneurs just because he liked the idea or the people, or worst of all, in his business, because he sympathizes with them, that may make him a great guy, but he won't stay in business for long.

If before investing, however, Chuck undertakes a rigorous series of checks, the odds of him losing his money become very much smaller. And the prospect of him getting a good return on his investment becomes very much higher.

So in Part I, we examine how Chuck would go about doing some systematic checking on you and your job or business. Chuck is looking for answers to one basic question, and one supplementary. The basic question is: *Are you likely to achieve your plans in your current job or business over the next few years?*

And the supplementary: *Do the opportunities to beat your plan surpass the risks of you not making your plan?*

The first thing Chuck needs to do is figure out what exactly your "business" is and what plans you have for the future.

*We can achieve what we want to
conceive and believe.*—Mark Twain

1 What's Your "Business"?

We know what we are, but know not what we may be.—William Shakespeare, *Hamlet*

What services do you offer, to whom? And which service to which customer group counts for most in your business?

Your backer needs to know this information because he hates wasting time. He wants to focus his time and effort researching those parts of your business that are the most important. There is little point in him spending hours checking out a service you offer to a customer group that only contributes to 1 percent of your sales. He wants to put in the work on the 80 percent.

This first step is relatively straightforward for the self-employed. But if you're an employee you need a little more imagination. We'll start with the self-employed, but employees need to read this section too.

If You're Self-Employed

As a business, what services, or less frequently in today's world, products do you offer? Most self-employed people tend to offer a number of services. These are typically related to each other, but each one is distinct, usually with different competitors.

Most self-employed people also tend to serve more than one customer group, typically reachable through different marketing routes.

Which service to which customer group brings in most of your income? This is your main "business chunk." And it's this chunk that Chuck Cash will be focusing his research on.

Or is it? Which service to which customer group is going to be most important to your business over the *next* three to five years? The same as over the *last* few years? If it's a different chunk, then that's the one Chuck will need to work on. Possibly in addition to the former chunk.

But what if you're not currently self-employed, but work as an employee in a company or other organization, large or small?

If You're an Employee

Just a reminder. This book is a step-by-step guide and works just as well for an employee as it does for a self-employed businessperson. But first you have to think of yourself as self-employed, as a business. As if you were outsourced.

Think of your whole earnings package, including wage or salary, vacation, sickness benefits, medical insurance, pension contribution, etc, as *revenues* for your business. What services are you providing to your organization to merit those revenues? Which people or groups of people in your organization find your services so useful they are prepared to pay those revenues for them?

That's it then. You're a "business"! You provide services and you have "customers." All you have to do is carve up the main tasks you undertake in your job into distinct services. Then, if appropriate, carve up the people who use your services into customer groups. That will show you which business chunk is currently most important to your business. And what about over the next three to five years? Will a different chunk become more important?

What Are Your Plans in Your Current Job or Business?

Suppose you're still in the same job or business in three or five years' time. Are you likely to be focusing on the same business chunks? How do you expect your income to develop over that time? What are your plans? It's these plans which need to be assessed in Part I of this book.

Some readers will have quite clear plans, and are reading this book as a "sanity check." It will help you to assess how achievable your plans are, whether you would back U in these plans and how you can make yourself more backable.

Many—probably most—readers will be uncertain of what their plans are and that is why they are reading this book. If that's you—and you currently have no concrete plans to develop your positioning in your company, or to reshape your business—then let's assume for now that *things stay more or less as they are now.*

Sure, as an employee, you may hope to receive some additional responsibility, a promotion, a pay rise (hopefully above inflation). Sure, as a self-employed person, you may hope to win some new customers and grow the business somewhat. But if you have no specific plans, let's for the time being assume that your "plan" for your job or business in five years' time is a steady, unspectacular improvement on what it is today.

The advantage of this assumption is its clarity. Because after you've worked through Part I of this book, you'll have a much firmer idea of whether just staying where you are today is a realistic scenario. Will you thrive in this same job or business in five years' time?

Cheryl's Business

Cheryl is one of two coaches at the Pines Lawn Tennis Club in Colorado Springs. She's not employed by the club, but gets paid directly by her clients. She's also coach to the third women's tennis team at Colorado Springs State University (CSSU), from whom she receives a regular pay check. And she coaches little ones at lunchtime tennis clubs at two elementary schools in the neighborhood.

Cheryl's other favorite sport is soccer and she coaches an Under 16 girls' soccer club, the Palmer Pumas, which trains on Saturday mornings at Palmer Park and plays in the Colorado Youth Soccer League on Sunday mornings. After these matches, Cheryl typically has to rush back to the Pines to attend to her tennis clients. It keeps her fit.

She's looking for backing from Chuck Cash. The first thing Chuck needs to do is find out what business she's in. He takes a look at her revenues over the last couple of years and finds that 66 percent has come from tennis clients at the Pines, 18 percent from CSSU, 4 percent from elementary schools, and 12 percent from her soccer client, the Palmer Pumas.

Chuck figures initially that he should focus his research on tennis coaching, rather than soccer coaching, and in particular her prospects as tennis coach at the Pines.

But Cheryl has other plans. She thinks she's found a gap in the market. In the Palmer Park area, the Colorado Youth Soccer League is strong and highly popular with youngsters. But it's quite a commitment. From the Under 8s to the Under 18s, kids are required to train on a Saturday morning and play matches, at home or away, on Sunday mornings. Cheryl knows that many girls who are good enough for her Under 16s are unable to register because they have other commitments on Sunday mornings, whether church, family, other activities, or just taking it easy. She also knows that many parents of younger kids in particular would love to have some organized structure for training and playing a game, but are not interested in the highly competitive aspect of a Sunday league.

To address this, Cheryl is thinking of setting up a club called Kickabout. It would be held on Wednesday evenings and Saturday mornings. Kids would be put into age groups, the youngest for 3½ to 5 year olds and the oldest from 10 to 11½ year olds. Each age group would be slotted into 45-minute time slots on a Saturday morning, and likewise for all except the youngest age group on Wednesday evenings. The latter sessions would be outside in Palmer Park during the summer and indoors at Knob Hill High School Sports Hall during winter.

Cheryl thinks that after a year or two she could get 20 to 30 kids in the youngest age group, but up to 50 kids in what's likely to be the most popular age group, the 6 to 7½ year olds. She envisages subcontracting seven or eight part-time soccer coaches.

If Kickabout comes off, Cheryl will have to drop coaching the Palmer Pumas, but she should be able to rearrange her coaching times at the Pines. And if Kickabout succeeds, her revenues over the next few years could rise to half as much again. Revenues from tennis clients at the Pines wouldn't change, but they would come down as a share of her overall revenues to around 50 percent. Kickabout would contribute more than a third.

If Chuck were to research only Cheryl's tennis coaching business, as he initially thought, he'd only be able to get comfortable with roughly half of Cheryl's future business. So how could he decide on whether to back her? Clearly he'll have to do as much research on kids' soccer coaching as on tennis coaching.

Debi's "Business"

Debi, our receptionist employed at a publishing firm, laughed when Chuck asked her to think of herself as a revenue-generating business. "Who'd pay for me?" she quipped. But her colleagues do pay, in effect. The business winners and deliverers in her firm generate the revenues that pay the wages and benefits of her and all other support staff.

Debi figured that over the last year about 80 percent of her time was spent on being a receptionist and the balance on acting as a marketing assistant. But what she'd really like over the next few years would be to spend at least 50 percent of her time as a marketing assistant, and one day maybe even drop the reception work altogether.

Whether she's to spend 50 or 100 percent of her time as a marketing assistant, Chuck will have to take a look not just at Debi's "business" as a receptionist, but also as a marketing assistant. He'll have to look at two business chunks.

In Short

What is your main business chunk (or chunks)?

What plans do you have over the next few years?

2 Where's Market Demand Going?

It's better to be in a market with the wind behind you than in your face.—Unattributed, but common quote in business world

You are not alone. There are others out there who do what you do. This chapter asks you to think about how market demand for *all* these people, including you, has changed in the last few years and how it is likely to change in the future. Will demand for you all grow?

Again, if you're an employee, it will help if you think of yourself as a business. You need to consider what will happen to demand for your kind of services over the next few years. That's demand for your services not just within your current company but *overall demand for your type of services across all organizations.*

Remember this: You have a better chance of prospering in a market that's growing than in one that's shrinking. Your backer knows this only too well.

How to Find Out?

You need to do some basic research. Try looking beyond your immediate catchment area at broader regional or national trends in the market for your services. It's easier to find information, and you can deduce later the extent to which broader trends are applicable to your catchment area.

Doing basic market research is a breeze these days. All you have to do is switch on your laptop, click onto your Internet connection, pop into Google or Yahoo, and type in your market alongside such words as "market," "growth," "forecasts," "trends."

You'll find that your search engine comes up with hundreds—maybe thousands—of websites to visit. Most of them will be irrelevant. One, two, or more will be spot on. You'll begrudge having to waste time trawling through dozens of useless sites, but hang on! Think of the hours of effort you're saving compared to the old days. Open up a Word file, and whenever you come across an article on a website that seems useful, copy it and drop it into your document.

You may well need to supplement your Googling with information gleaned locally, whether from the local press or a few discrete telephone calls with those in the know. You are weaving your own web of information on your market.

What's Driving Demand?

To understand whether a market is going to grow in the future, you have to understand what the underlying influences are and how they may change.

The factors that influence a market are called demand drivers. Typical drivers include growth in per capita income, population growth, government policy, changing levels of awareness, price change, fashion (even a craze), and weather.

All you have to do is this. Step 1: Find out how market demand has been growing in the past. Step 2: Assess what drivers have been influencing this past growth. Step 3: Think how these drivers may change in influence in the future—or whether new drivers will become influential. And, finally, Step 4: Forecast future demand.

Don't worry if you can't find any numbers, any growth rates. Great if you can, but very often the numbers for your particular market niche won't exist. What you need to get at is trends. Find out whether the market for your type of services has been growing fast, growing slowly, holding flat, declining slowly or declining fast. That's all you need.

Let's take a simple example. You're offering a relatively new service to the elderly. Step 1: You find that the market has been growing at 5 to 10 percent per year over the last few years. Step 2: You identify the main drivers as (a) per capita income growth, (b) growth in the elderly population, and (c) growing awareness of the service by elderly people. Step 3: You believe income growth will continue as before, the elderly population will grow even faster in the future, and that awareness can only get more widespread. Step 4: You conclude that growth in your market will accelerate and could reach over 10 percent per year over the next few years. Simple!

Employees Need to Check Market Demand at Two Levels

So far we've looked only at market demand prospects for self-employed people. If you're an employee, the approach is similar but a little more complicated. You need to look at market demand prospects at two levels:

- At the level of the economy (local, regional, or national, as for the self-employed, depending on your willingness—or ability—to relocate)—Where's overall market demand for your type of services heading?
- At the level of your company—Where's demand for your type of services heading *within your company?*

Your backer needs to know how employable you would be if things go wrong in your current company or organization and you need to leave. This could be for a variety of reasons. It could involve personality conflict. Your boss may move on and you don't get on with the new one. Maybe an ingratiating colleague is promoted undeservingly above you. It might be that you can't tolerate working in the same room as a colleague. Companies are essentially

---

Dubious Divination

In 1995, an unemployed, welfare-dependent, clinically depressed, single mother tried desperately to interest the British publishing community in her manuscript about a teenage wizard. Much of the book had been written in warm, cozy cafes, the author having walked briskly through the crisp Edinburgh air to lull her daughter to sleep. A dozen publishers turned her down. In a Britain poised to embrace a New Labour government, perhaps they saw no market demand for a book about a boarding school for witches and wizards. Poor call, guys—just be careful next time you're in a dark alleyway and bump into a lad with specs and a scar on his forehead muttering *Furnunculus, Rictusempra,* or *Tarantallegra...*

---

gatherings of people. People fall out. You may be forced to leave your company even though you do your job extremely well and everyone knows it.

But there's another reason. If there's a chance that your company gets into trouble—performing poorly relative to the competition—then that could have a major impact on the *demand by your company for your type of services.* If your company is forced to restructure, then you and your colleagues may face a program of layoffs. If the worst happens, and your company closes down, then you and your fellow service providers will find yourselves on the labor market all at the same time. Not a good place to be.

If, however, your company is performing well, and from what you can tell, better than most of the competition, then that's good news. Demand in your company for your type of service is likely to be higher than overall market demand.

Cheryl's Market Demand Prospects

It took Chuck Cash less than five minutes of Googling to find out that tennis was a growth sport. A survey by the U.S. Tennis Association and the Tennis Industry Association found that 25 million Americans played tennis in 2005, an increase of 4 percent from 2004. The number of "frequent" players (>21 times/year) jumped by 9 percent to top 5 million. Growth was supported by other indicators, such as increases in racquet sales, tennis ball sales, television ratings, and attendance at pro tournaments.

Chuck found that the main driver was desire for a more active and healthy lifestyle. Growth was also being boosted by a range of USTA programs to encourage participation—including promotion and positioning of the sport as "fun, social, healthy, inclusive, accessible, and affordable." Each of these drivers seemed set to remain influential, implying further steady growth in the tennis playing population.

Chuck found even more encouraging information on soccer playing. The number of players in high school soccer teams grew at over 5 percent a year between 1991 and 2004, with girls accounting for a staggering 47 percent. Soccer had also grown rapidly at NCAA colleges, with a trebling of female players since 1991.Total U.S. soccer participation had reached 18 million, catching up to tennis numbers.

Drivers of this growth were the low cost of participation, growing awareness, interest in international soccer games on TV, and again, demands for a healthier, more active lifestyle. These seemed set to strengthen, especially awareness. Chuck figured he was looking at a market with quite some growth left in it.

That wasn't the end of the story though. Just because more people were playing sport, it didn't necessarily mean that market demand for *coaching* would be growing at the same rate. Soccer, after all, is a game that can be played in any park at any time by any number of players. Could Chuck be sure that there was no adverse trend of people teaching themselves and preferring to do without coaches? Or could it be the opposite—that as people get better off they are more prepared to pay for the services of a coach, whether through group classes or individual tuition? A bit more Googling, some data from coaching association websites and Chuck concluded that national demand for both tennis and soccer coaching was steadily rising.

Then there was one final, important element to consider. What about any local or regional peculiarities? Were the people of Colorado Springs any different from elsewhere in the country in their tennis- or soccer-playing habits? Were they more or less active? Were there competing sports that were particularly popular locally? Did Colorado Springs people differ in their attitude to engaging a coach?

Chuck needed to make just three local calls. The first was to one of the sports development officers with the Colorado state government. She told him that sport participation in Colorado Springs, home of the U.S. Olympic Training Center, was both higher and growing at least as fast as in the rest of the country. Demand for government-sponsored sports coaching initiatives for both youngsters and adults was buoyant. Both tennis and soccer were gaining in popularity, she thought, despite competition from so many other sports, many of whose national associations were based in the city (e.g., basketball, hockey, swimming).

A woman from the Colorado Springs Community Tennis Association confirmed that more tennis teams were being registered for USTA league tournaments, and a gentleman from the Colorado Springs Soccer Association believed that soccer participation in the area was growing, boosted, he thought, by the publicity around David Beckham's arrival at LA Galaxy.

Chuck felt comfortable. Tennis and soccer coaching in Colorado Springs seemed to be markets with the wind behind.

Debi's Market Demand Prospects

Market demand prospects didn't look so uniformly healthy for Debi. At the level of the firm, demand seemed fine, but at the level of the local economy things looked anything but. Over one third of the New York City economy is in the financial services sector, and the turmoil in financial markets sparked by the subprime mortgage crisis cast doubt on the whole sector's prospects in the short-term. Widespread redundancies seemed inevitable, not just among investment bankers, but also among clerical and related support staff. Overall market demand for receptionist and marketing personnel in New York City seemed poised to tighten. Debi and other receptionists in firms less affected by the financial meltdown would have to sit tight for a year or two.

Chuck had seen financial crises come and go. Once the dust had settled, New York would remain, along with London and Tokyo, one of the three pillars in global financial markets. Market demand for reception services, other things being equal, should recover in the medium term.

But what of these "other things"? Were there other drivers at work here? Could firms be using fewer receptionists in the information age? And marketing personnel? Chuck did some Googling and found that firms still employed as many receptionists as before, despite having added greatly to their security staff. And in marketing, there would surely be a contraction in spending and employment during the economic turmoil, but they seemed set to return to their slow trend growth curve once recovery took hold.

Finally, Chuck looked at the publishing sector, and at Little, Stamp in particular. He found that although New York publishing firms as a whole have lost market share to rival firms sprouting up all over the country, from Vermont to Oregon, they have expanded nevertheless on the back of sustained market growth in book and magazine publishing.

Chuck found that Little, Stamp, a medium-sized house still run by its founders, Charlie Little and Ian Stamp, had established a good, well-defined position in nonfiction publishing. It was especially well reputed in self-help, career, and business books, which were among the fastest growing segments in publishing. Chuck figured that Little, Stamp looked a safe bet as a long-term employer for Debi, despite the current economic gloom outside its front door.

In Short

How has market demand for your type of services grown in the last few years?

What factors drove that growth? How may they change?

3 What About the Competition?

Competition's a bitch—but that's how we get puppies.—Unattributed, heard in the world of finance

This chapter is in some ways unfortunate. Life would be a piece of cake if you were the only person who could provide your service, who could do your job. If your customers (or colleagues if you're an employee) had no choice but to come to you, you could shape your job to suit your own needs. And charge the customer what you wanted, within reason.

Life isn't like that. First, if a job's worth doing, there will be more than one of you wanting to do it. Second, none of us is irreplaceable. Don't kid yourself. There's always someone who can do any job just as well as you. A screenwriter may have a certain actress in mind when he creates a screen role, but there's no guarantee she'll be available or willing to take the part. And when the second or fourth choice wins the Oscar for Best Actress, who then remembers the actress for whom the role was initially created?

There's always competition. There are others out there, often many others, who are either doing, or may be thinking of doing, what you're doing. What you need to think about is whether competition is actually going to get *tougher*. Whatever your competitive situation today, it results in you making a profit or earning a salary of however many thousand dollars a year. But that's today. What your backer needs to know is what's going to happen *tomorrow*. Will the competitive environment enable you to continue to make that income, or grow it in line with your plans, in three or five years' time?

Above all, is there any chance that there may be too many of you competing for the same jobs or business in the future?

Who's the Competition?

First, you need to be clear about who your competitors are. Think about when you provide a particular service to a particularly good customer. Who else could she have gone to? Think about all your services to all your customers. What other names frequently crop up—who do they go to, or who could they have gone to? They're your competition.

If you provide a service to local residents, but many of your clients are prepared to travel some distance to another provider, then that provider is as much a competitor as the provider down the road.

If you're an employee, it's a little trickier to figure out who your competitors are, but it can be quite revealing. Your competitors are not just your fellow employees who do the same job as you. They are also your fellow employees who could and would like to do the same job as you. And they are the independent contractors who could be engaged by your boss to do your job temporarily. Or they could be engaged on a longer-term basis should your company decide to outsource your job.

Finally, your potential competitors are all those in the marketplace who are doing similar jobs at other companies and would apply for your job if they knew there were a vacancy. Or who might apply on spec anyway. These are all your competitors!

How Tough Is Competition in Your Market?

How competitive is your market? Markets tend to be tough when:

- There are many providers of your type of service.
- The number of providers is growing slowly (toughest when numbers are declining)
- The market is unregulated by government, trade unions, or professional associations.
- There are low barriers to entry, like qualifications, training, or experience
- Your type of service can be substituted (possibly by technological change)
- There are few buyers compared to the number of providers.

How tough is competition in your market? Is it poised to get tougher? Or is it more likely to stay the same? Could it even ease up?

Market Balance, Prices, and Earnings

You looked at market demand prospects in the last chapter and at competition in this chapter. You should now have some idea of whether market demand and market supply are likely to be in balance over the next few years.

If so, then prices for your services may well continue to rise as they have in the recent past—probably along with inflation, just above or just below.

If, however, your market is due to move from balance to oversupply—where supply exceeds demand—that will place a dampener on prices. You and your competitors will have to fight more fiercely for custom, and any planned price increases to meet rising costs may have to be put on hold.

Likewise, if you're an employee, it's unlikely that you and your colleagues will receive a significant salary increase if your company is facing oversupply in the market and not enough market demand. Conversely, in times of excess demand and your company has an overflowing order book, that's when you stand a good chance of pushing through a hike in salary or bonus.

Cheryl's Competition

Chuck asks Cheryl who her competitors are. Instinctively, she thinks of formidable competitors to the Pines Lawn Tennis Club, where she works, such as the Colorado Springs Racquets Club or even the Cheyenne Mountain Country Club out of town. The latter,

Love Me Do

Suppose you were a producer in the recording company Parlaphone in the spring of 1962. You had just held an audition for four high-spirited young lads from Liverpool. They were okay as singers and musicians, but nothing exceptional. Competition was intense; there were so many wannabe rock 'n' roll groups around, a dozen in Liverpool alone. Backing a group was high cost and high risk. It was no surprise that these lads had been turned down by other studios. Yet they had come up with a catchy name, sported a whacky mop-top look and oozed charisma. You had a hunch and backed them. Baby, you're a rich man...

P.S. A prominent record producer of the time believed that market demand for Buddy Holly style beat-groups was on the wane. That they were a fad of the 1950s. Boy, you're going to carry that weight...

for example, in addition to its fabulous golf, swimming, sailing, and fishing facilities, has 12 outdoor and 6 indoor tennis courts. This compares with the Pines' eight plexicushion acrylic hard courts, only one of which is floodlit.

The Country Club employs three full-time tennis professionals who must be regarded as direct competitors of Cheryl. Likewise the three at the Racquets Club, two more at Colorado Springs State University, and some more at a couple of other smaller clubs. But Cheryl's colleague, George, who's the head coach at the Pines, is also a competitor. As is Cheryl's buddy, Concha, who coaches at the public courts down the road. Then there are coaches at the other public courts, at the town's 20 or so public high schools, at the private schools, and so on. In all, and allowing for part-time coaches, Cheryl thinks there must be 25 to 30 tennis coaches active in the Colorado Springs area competing for the same customer base she aims to serve.

Then there's the soccer. Aside from the hosts of dads, moms, and granddads ardently putting their kids through their paces in the public parks, there are around 60 trained coaches in Colorado Springs registered with the Colorado Soccer Association. Cheryl is but one of them. As for Cheryl's plans for Kickabout, there's nothing really comparable in Colorado Springs, but Cheryl got her idea from a similar venture in a suburb of the state capital, Denver.

So how will competition shape up over the next few years? Chuck and Cheryl went through the checklist. The number of coaches had been growing, but seemingly in line with demand growth. There may be some threat from new entrants in soccer coaching, more so than in tennis since it was easier to register in soccer. But that had always been the case and as long as the market kept growing, they didn't expect that to be a problem.

Sure there was a threat of substitution—Americans, or just Coloradans, may switch from tennis and soccer to, say, beach volleyball and rugby, but there were no signs of that as yet. And yes, customers wielded a lot of power. If they weren't satisfied with Cheryl at the Pines, they could easily switch to George, Concha, or many others.

Overall, Chuck concluded that the tennis coaching market in Colorado Springs was of medium competitiveness, with the possibility of some toughening over the years if demand growth tailed off. Soccer coaching he found to be of medium/high competitiveness because of the lower entry barriers, but unlikely to get much tougher.

Competitive analysis for Cheryl's proposed new venture, Kickabout, was trickier, since there was no direct competitor. There was plenty of indirect competition, such as the elementary school teams and the youth league teams, but the nearest direct equivalent was in Denver. Chuck concluded that competitive intensity was likely to be low/medium. Time to look in more detail at what Cheryl was planning to offer.

Debi's Competition

Debi's competition is threefold. Most immediately, there are the other two receptionists at Little, Stamp—the extrovert and occasionally outrageous Rosita and the calm, mature, but quick-witted Valerie. Then there are the receptionists from the temping agencies that are used now and again when one of the full-timers is sick or on vacation. And there are all those receptionists or would-be receptionists employed elsewhere in New York City, or currently in between jobs, or employed out of town but hoping to move to the Big Apple, or currently in other occupations but wishing to switch to receptionist work, who might be tempted to apply for a receptionist vacancy at Little, Stamp should one arise. In other words, Debi's competition effectively encompasses the entire receptionist labor force active or potentially active in New York City.

The same applies to Debi's plans to move into marketing. For the word "receptionist" in the above paragraph, read "marketing assistant." Debi is effectively in competition with the entire marketing assistant labor force active or potentially active in New York City.

Chuck took Debi through the checklist. Both the receptionist and marketing assistant markets had plenty of players but some long-term trend demand growth. Both occupations were viewed as attractive to applicants of medium levels of educational achievement and had low entry barriers, so there was a high threat of new entrants. Overall, they were markets of medium/high competitive intensity.

But this was set to change. The fallout from the 2007–2009 financial meltdown would see scores of receptionists and marketing assistants out of work. Many of these would come knocking on the door of Little, Stamp. This could have an impact, if not on Debi's job tenure, then on her wage levels over the next couple of years. Chuck concluded that competitive intensity was currently high and would get higher before returning to its long-term medium/high level with eventual New York–spirit economic bounce-back.

In Short

Will competition in your marketplace get tougher over the next few years?

Any chance of too many people competing for your job or business?

What implications for growth in prices or earnings?

4 What Do Customers Need?

"It is not your aptitude, but your attitude, that determines your altitude"—Zig Ziglar

What do customers need from providers such as you? If you're an employee, what do your managers need from you and your peers?

Customer needs for the self-employed can be usefully grouped into six categories— effectiveness, efficiency, relationship, range, premises (if applicable), and price. They can be conveniently remembered, in deference to a cult science fiction movie, as the *E2-R2-P2* of customer needs.

Likewise "customer" needs of employees fall more or less into the same categories. Your managers expect from you the appropriate balance of service and price (that is, salary and benefits). But they provide the premises. Let's look at each in turn.

E1: Effectiveness. The customer wants the job done. Not half-done, not over-done, just done. She will have expectations of the service provider concerning skills, knowledge and experience to get that job done. These expectations will be higher depending on the importance of the service to the customer. A young man seeking a crew cut will have less demanding needs of his barber than one who wants the cool cut sported by some movie star. A patient's needs of her heart surgeon will be more demanding than those of her physio-therapist.

E2: Efficiency. The customer wants the job done on time. All customers place some level of importance on efficiency for all types of service. You may not care if your crew cut takes 10, 15, even 30 minutes, but you would care if it took all Saturday afternoon and you missed the big football game.

R1: Relationship. A barber gives a good crew cut and he does it quickly. But do you like the guy? Is he the sort of guy you feel comfort-able with having his hands on your head? Do you want your barber to chat or stay quiet? Does it matter to you if this guy seems bored and disinterested?

Customers expect the right *attitude* in their service provider. A positive attitude brings with it enthusiasm, cheer, conviviality, optimism, humor, energy, effort, and other uplifting at-tributes. It can leave the customer feeling she has received exceptional value from the service.

A negative attitude, bringing grumpiness, gloom, pessimism, seriousness, lethargy, and other down-spiriting attributes, can leave the cus-tomer feeling glad to be rid of the service provider.

A negative attitude may be the result of dissatisfaction with the job. If this is so for you, your attitude may impinge on your ability to do the job (see Chapter 6). And you may need to consider changing careers, perhaps following your passion (see Part III).

R2: Range. This is an area customers can find important for some services, even most important, and for other services of no importance at all. Does your barber also offer head massage? Do you care?

P1: Premises. This can be important for some self-employed people. Hair stylists, travel agents, and shopkeepers, for example, need a storefront. Location and décor should be appropriate for the pocket of the target customer.

P2: Price. For nonessential services, we tend to be price sensitive. When your eight-year-old son's hair is flopping over his eyes, you look for a barber. He has little interest in his appearance (for the time being!), so you may look around for the cheapest. But how cheap are you prepared to go? Would you take him to a barber's that is (literally) dirt cheap, where the combs are greasy, the floor is covered with hair, and the barber is a miserable so-and-so? Probably not. You set minimum standards of service and then go for a reasonable price.

For essential services, we tend to be less fixated with price. When your central heating system breaks down in the middle of winter, will you go for the cheapest service engineer? Or will you call around your friends and acquaintances to find someone who is reliable, arrives when he says he will, fixes it with no fuss, and charges a price that is not exactly cheap but at least is no rip-off?

That's all very well in theory, you may ask, but how do you know what customers want? Simple. Ask them!

It doesn't take long. You'd be surprised how after just a few discussions a predictable pattern begins to emerge. Some may consider one need "very important," others just "important." But it's seldom that another will consider that need "unimportant." Customers within a particular business chunk tend to have similar needs.

This is one step that is much easier for the employee. Most employees have regular reviews with their managers, at least once a year when it's pay raise time. Your boss will tell you what she needs from you and your colleagues.

One more thing. While you're talking to your customers, or to your managers, find out how their needs are likely to *change in the future*. If they think that one need is very important to them now, will it remain as important in a few years' time? You need to know.

Customer Needs in Cheryl's Business

What do customers need from a tennis and soccer coach like Cheryl? She asks them. She finds that all customers expect their coach to be proficient at the sport in question. To be an effective role model, that's customer need number one.

Cheryl finds another need rated as very important, and that is relationship. Customers expect their coaches to be personable, to have an upbeat attitude and to be able to communicate effectively.

Other important needs are efficiency (arriving on time, delivering the appropriate coaching within the allotted timeframe etc) and price—important, but not very important, as long as the fees come in the right ball park.

Range isn't a major need. Her tennis customers are often intrigued that Cheryl also coaches soccer, but it's no factor in their decision to engage her.

One customer need under the effectiveness (E1) heading that is very important for soccer coaching, but less so for tennis, is control. Customers expect the coach to be able to control, motivate, and if necessary, discipline a group of potentially unruly youngsters.

Cheryl doesn't see these customer needs changing much over time. But she recognizes that a different range of capabilities will be needed to meet customer needs when running a venture such as Kickabout. This she'll discuss with Chuck Cash in the next chapter.

"Customer" Needs in Debi's Job

What do Debi's "customers," in other words her bosses, require from the reception services of her and her colleagues, or indeed of external, subcontracted suppliers? Debi believes that most important is relationship—rapport with both client and colleague as they come through the door and over the telephone, and a generally upbeat attitude. Also important is organizational reliability—taking messages, passing them on effectively, taking on projects devolved to her by PAs and marketing staff—for example, finding a venue for the Christmas party. And efficiency—the office relies on its receptionists to be punctual. Less important are knowledge, experience, range, and price.

Debi thinks customer needs from marketing assistant services are similar but with a different emphasis. Instead of relationship being rated as of high importance and organizational reliability medium, it will be vice versa for marketing services. In other words, if Debi were to move to the marketing department, there would be rather less call for her relationship skills and more for her organizational skills. We'll return to this shift of emphasis in the next chapter.

In Short

What do customers need from your type of service?

How important are each of the E2-R2-P2 of customer needs? Attitude?

How will these needs change in importance over time?

5 What Do You Need to Do to Succeed?

If you can't change your fate, change your attitude.—Amy Tan

In the last chapter we looked at what customers need from providers of your services. In this chapter, we'll look at what providers like you need to do to meet those needs and run a successful business, if you're self-employed, or progress successfully in your job, if you're an employee.

First, let's be clear about what Part I of this book is trying to do. And what it's not. Here we're defining "success," for the time being, as being able to bring home the kind of earnings you've envisioned in your business plan. It's a narrow definition, but it's the only one of interest or use to Chuck Cash.

Of course, this begs questions regarding job satisfaction and job fulfillment. These we'll return to in Parts II and III. For the time being, however, Chuck is not particularly interested in, for example, how meaningful your work is—*unless any dissatisfaction is going to impair your performance.* Then he's going to be very interested, and concerned.

Most of the things you need to get right will relate to the skills and attributes, *or capabilities,* required of *an individual person* providing your type of service. Not all though. If you're self-employed, factors such as the range and skills of your subcontractors, or location and standard of premises, relate to your business, not just to you as an individual.

We'll call them Key Kapabilities, or K2s for short. Not to be confused with the second highest mountain in the world, Mount K2 of the Karakoram range in the Himalayas, but the term may serve as a reminder of the peaks we may need to climb in order to succeed.

Converting Customer Needs Into Key Kapabilities

Conversion is fairly straightforward in most cases. An associated K2 can often seem similar to, even the same as, the customer need. Suppose, for example, that you as a customer want your hair stylist to be good at coloring. That's one of your needs. So the stylist needs to be skilled at coloring. That's a K2.

But K2s generally tend to take a different perspective from customer needs. Here's an example. When you jump on the city tour bus in Acapulco, Rome, or Kyoto, you expect to be able to understand clearly what the tour guide is saying. The customer need is clarity of communication. The associated K2s are proficiency in the language of delivery and clear communication skills.

What do providers of your type of services need to do to meet customer needs? What are the associated K2s for each customer need in your business or job?

When converting a customer need, you may find that the associated K2 is the same as you've already associated with another customer need. In other words, one K2 can sometimes be sufficient to meet two or more customer needs. Returning to the tour guide, for example, another customer need may well be rapport with the guide. Rapport will be greatly eased through fluency in the language of delivery. In this example one K2, language proficiency, serves two customer needs, namely clarity of communication, and rapport.

There's one customer need that needs special attention, and that's price. Customers of most services expect a keen *price*. So the service providers need to keep their *costs* down. Price is a customer need, cost competitiveness a K2.

In a competitive service business like car repair, for example, middle income car owning customers tend to be sensitive to price, among other needs like quality of work and integrity. The self-employed car mechanic will therefore try and keep down his rental costs of premises by locating his garage well off the high street, maybe off the side streets too, and on some commercially-zoned land alongside the railway line.

Finally, you need to note how important each of these K2s is. If you rated the associated customer need as, for example, very important, so too will be that K2.

Other K2s: Management
and Market Share

So far, we've derived K2s from the customer needs set out in Chapter 4. There are two more important K2s to be considered, especially for the self-employed: management capabilities and market share.

Management-related K2s may be very important in your business. As a self-employed individual, you have to do every job, play every role in your business. You're chairman of the board, chief executive officer, chief finance officer, chief operating officer, sales director, marketing director, IT director, even company secretary, all rolled into one. The flipside is that you're also the gofer.

How important a K2 is management to your business? Above all, how important is sales and marketing to your business? Many self-employed or small businesses fail not because the individuals aren't competent at the service they offer. Quite the contrary. Very often they're the best and that's what gave them the confidence to break out on their own in the first place.

They fail because no one knows they're there. Sales and marketing are the lifeblood of the self-employed person, a major K2.

There's one final K2—an important one—that isn't directly derived from a customer need. This is the size of your presence in a particular business chunk—in other words, your share of that particular market.

Market share is an indicator of the breadth and depth of your customer relationships and your business reputation. Since it is more difficult to gain a new customer than to do repeat business with an existing customer, the provider with the larger market share typically has a competitive advantage—*the power of the incumbent.*

Take this example. If your hair stylist fulfills all your customer needs—excellent hair styling, relaxing premises, rapport (aka gossip!), and a reasonable price, the fact that one or two of your friends are chatting about the excellent new stylist who has just set up further down the street will not necessarily tempt you away from your usual provider. Why switch? Your stylist would be most upset, especially when she has done nothing to deserve such disloyalty. This is the power of the incumbent. Customers don't like switching, unless they are sorely tempted (the pull factor) or forced to move through deficient service (the push factor). Keep the service levels high and your customers will tend to stick with the service they know.

ATTENTION! Any Must-Have K2s?

There is one final wrinkle. But it may be crucial.

Is any one of your K2s so important that if you don't rank highly against it you shouldn't even be in the business or job? You simply won't begin to compete, let alone succeed? You won't win any business, or you won't be able to deliver on the business you win? In other words, it is a *must-have* K2, rather than a mere *should-have* K2.

Let's take an extreme example. Suppose Chuck Cash is thinking of backing Mr. Fayque, a locally respected psychotherapist working out of his smartly converted front room in a fashionable suburb of Tulsa, Oklahoma. Chuck finds that Mr. Fayque rates highly against all the major K2s. His customers feel comfortable in his grasp of techniques, he's immensely personable, and he has years of experience. There's just the one problem: He's not qualified! Chuck discovers that the framed certificate in pride of place in Mr. Fayque's front room is a fake. Qualification is a must-have K2. Chuck won't back him.

Are any of the K2s in your business or job must-haves? Keep a note of them before we assess your rating against all K2s in the next chapter.

Is Attitude a Must-Have K2?

How important is attitude in your job or business? Is it one of many should-have K2s or could it be a must-have K2?

Imagine dropping off your 12-year-old daughter at a summer camp in the Rockies and being "greeted" by a couple of camp staff wearing disinterested or downright miserable faces. You'd stuff your daughter back in the car, do a u-turn, and head for home. An enthusiastic, cheerful attitude is a must-have in the summer camp business. Likewise in most leisure, travel, and entertainment businesses—think how many people would carry on watching *American Idol* if Simon Cowell never cracked a toothy smile after one of his pompous but telling putdowns!

Attitude is a must-have in Cheryl's sports coaching business. Without a cheerful, enthusiastic, even passionate approach to her job, customers would go elsewhere. Period. It should also be a must-have in Debi's line of work. Yet I'm sure we've all come across receptionists who have a bored, disinterested attitude. Think how you as an aspiring author would feel if you walked into Little, Stamp to find a receptionist reading her celebrity magazine, finally raising her head to say in a bored tone, "So how can I help *you?*," the final word dripping in disdain. I suspect you'd look elsewhere for a publisher!

K2s in Cheryl's Business

What K2s do sports coaches like Cheryl need? Well, she has already identified the main customer needs, namely competence at playing the sport, a good relationship with customers, and, for soccer, management and control of young people. She figures that the main corresponding K2s are as follows (with degree of importance in brackets):

- An ability to play the game competitively to at least club level, preferably state level (high)
- A personable character, with an upbeat attitude (high)
- Skills in communication (medium/high)
- Skills in people management and control—for soccer (high)

These seem pretty straightforward. But these are the K2s for being an individual sports coach. Will they be relevant for running a small coaching business like Kickabout? She consults with Chuck and she's relieved to hear that the K2s remain unchanged, but with a couple more added on:

- Skills in marketing the venture to the local community (high)
- Skills in managing and motivating subcontracted fellow coaches (medium/high)

Important, though perhaps not as important, Chuck tells Cheryl, will be general skills in managing a small business. Not too daunting, Cheryl thinks. We'll see in the next chapter how Chuck rates Cheryl against these K2s...

K2s in Debi's Job

Debi has found that the main "customer" needs for reception services at Little, Stamp are a good relationship with the company's clients, organizational reliability, and efficiency. Against these needs, Debi places these corresponding K2s:

- A personable character, with an upbeat attitude (high)
- Communication skills (high)
- Organizational skills (medium/high)
- Time management skills (medium)

Chuck agrees with Debi's findings. Then they discuss how these K2s may differ in the market for marketing assistant services, as follows:

- Organizational skills (high)

- Marketing training (high)
- A personable character, with an upbeat attitude (medium)
- Skills in communication (medium)
- Time management skills (medium)

For the most part, these are the same K2s, they conclude, but with a different ranking in emphasis. "So, is this for you?" Chuck asks. Debi replies that she'll think some more about it—and we'll see where she comes to in Chapter 6.

In Short

What Key Kababilities (K2s) should providers like you have to meet customer needs?

How important is management or market share?

Any must-have K2s? Attitude?

6 How Do YOU Measure Up?

*I'm not offended by dumb blonde jokes
because I know that I'm not dumb. I also know
I'm not blonde.*—Dolly Parton

In the last chapter you figured out what people need to do to succeed in your type of service. Here we'll see how you measure up, how you rate against the Key Kapabilities needed for success. And how your competitors rate.

This is the easy part. You've done the hard graft in the last couple of chapters, paving the way for the show-down of this chapter.

It may also be the fun part. You may be pleasantly surprised at how well you rate against your peers.

But it may also be the shocking part. You may find that you're poorly placed to compete or even survive in the competitive arena in which you play. Your backer may back *off*, rather than back *U!*—in which case, you may need to move swiftly to Part III of this book!

How Do You Rate Against Each K2?

All you need to do is rate yourself against each of the K2s drawn up in the last chapter. There are a number of ways you can rate yourself—for instance with numbers, ticks, or words. I prefer the numbers method, but that's a tad more technical and is set out in detail in this book's big sister, *Backing U!* A words approach seems more appropriate for this *LITE* version. It should get us to the same answer.

For each K2, assess whether you perform more or less as well as other players in your market. If so, give yourself a *favorable* rating against that K2. Or do you think you perform better than most, worthy of a *strong* rating? Best of all, do you think you merit a *very strong* rating against that K2?

Or do you feel you don't measure up quite so well against the competition in that K2? Do you feel you're okay, but perhaps a bit below the average player, so you're worth just an *okay-ish* rating? Worst of all, do you feel that in that K2 you are way behind the others, so all you get is a *weak* rating?

Now do the same for each of your competitors against each K2. Which competitor performs best against this K2? Does she merit a *very strong,* or is she better but not *that* much better than everyone else, for a *strong?* And what about that guy down the road, does he barely merit an *okay-ish* against that K2? And so on against each K2 for each main competitor...

What's Your Overall K2 Rating?

Now you can assess your overall K2 rating. This is a measure of how well you compete in your marketplace. It measures how competitive you are against your peers, against all those in your marketplace providing the same type of service as you.

To do this, you need to remember the degree of importance you attached to each of the K2s. They are not of equal importance. Some are more important than others. So first take a look at how you rated yourself against the *most important* K2s. Those are the ratings that really count. Then see how you rated against the K2s of medium/high importance, and so on down.

Put them all together and how do you rate overall? Is your overall competitiveness, your overall K2 rating, *favorable?* Is it, hopefully, *strong?* Somewhere in between, like *favorable/ strong?* Maybe even *strong/very strong?*

Or is your overall K2 rating below average? Is it just *okay-ish,* or *okay-ish/favorable?* If so, which K2 has dragged down your overall performance?

And what about your competitors? What are their overall K2 ratings? Remember again to take into account the relative importance of each K2 before deducing overall ratings. Who's the strongest? The weakest? Where do you sit?

How to Find Out?

Finding out your K2 ratings is easy for employees. Ask your boss! Or wait until your next review comes along and ask her then. You could even try asking her which of your peers she thinks rates most highly against each K2, although she might be a bit hesitant revealing this. Ask her how you should go about improving your performance against one or two of the K2s.

For the self-employed, the first step is to do it yourself. Over the years, or months if you've only just started, you'll already have had some occasional feedback from your customers: "Great piece of work" generally means you've done something right. "No way am I gonna pay you for that!" suggests the opposite.

Have a go at rating yourself. Then stick a question mark against those ratings where you're a little unsure on how you perform. Investigate those ratings one or two at a time. Next time you're with a customer, throw in the line: "By the way, you know that job I did for you a couple of months ago—were you happy with the turnaround time? Did you expect it to be quicker?" Gradually you'll be able to start removing the question marks and firm up your performance rating.

While rating your own performance, you should also of course be rating those of your competitors. Try throwing in the odd question to your customers about your competitors, like: "What about Joe? Does he turn things round as fast as I do?" Gradually the question marks on your competitors' ratings should also disappear.

A Dollop of Talent

Imagine you're an investor in Nashville, Tennessee, in 1964 and a girl from upcountry walks into your office. She's the ("dirt poor") fourth of 12 siblings, all living in a one-room cabin on the slopes of the Great Smoky Mountains. She has just been signed by a record label to sing bubblegum pop, but that's not where her passion lies. She wants your backing to sing country music ("If you talk bad about country music, it's like saying bad things about my momma. Them's fightin' words."). You weigh up her K2 rating. She certainly looks distinctive ("I modeled my looks on the town tramp."), with assets appealing to a male audience ("I was the first woman to burn my bra; it took the fire department four days to put it out!"). But it's the raw talent that grabs you. This is a girl with a voice, who writes her own songs and plays the guitar, banjo, piano and a bunch of other instruments. You're not to know that one day she'll be so smart a businesswoman she won't sign away the rights of "I Will Always Love You," even to Elvis. But you do know that her K2 rating looks good in a market that's going places. She's a "9 to 5" bet.

How May Your K2 Rating Improve Over the Next Few Years?

So far your K2 rating has been static. You've rated your competitiveness now, as things are today. But that's only the first part of the story. Your backer also needs to know how your position may change over the next few years. He'll want to understand the dynamics. Is it set to improve, or worsen?

Do you have plans to improve against some K2s? Any prospective improvements need, for the time being, to be both in the pipeline *and* likely, for your backer to be convinced.

One obvious area where you may well improve your rating is in experience, since you will by then be three years' more experienced. If you already have 20 years' experience, an extra three years won't make much difference. But if you've only had 20 months' experience, an extra 36 could well make a big difference.

Other areas of potential improvement may be in skills or qualifications. If you're set to undergo any further training, then that should be factored in. Remember though that K2 improvement is a double-edged sword. Your competitors too may have plans. They too will be more experienced in three years' time. They too may upgrade their skills or qualifications. Do you have any idea what they're planning to do to improve their competitiveness in the near future? What could they do? *What are you afraid they'll do?*

Any Chance You Won't Get Past First Base?

In the last chapter, we introduced the concept of the must-have K2—without a good rating in which a provider cannot even begin to compete.

Did you find a must-have K2 in any of your business chunks? If so, how do you rate against it? *Favorable, strong?* Fine. *Okay-ish?* Questionable. *Weak?* Troublesome. You're probably out. You don't get past first base.

And what about in a few years' time? Will any of the K2s have become a must-have? How you will you rate then? Will you still get past first base?

And even though you rate *okay-ish* against a must-have K2 today, is there any chance of your rating slipping over time? Could it slide into tricky territory?

Is attitude a must-have K2 in your job or business? How's yours? How will it be in a few years' time?

This may be a case of being cruel to be kind. It's better to know. The sooner you realize that you're in the wrong business, or job, the sooner you can move on. Part III can help you with that.

Cheryl's K2 Rating

It was easy for Cheryl to find out the ratings she was after. She often has a leisurely chat with the last client of the day while they are packing away the rackets, and she could deftly steer the conversation toward feedback. Likewise, she found plenty of opportunity to talk to some of the girls at the Palmer Pumas and their parents, especially after Saturday morning training.

Her results were a touch surprising but rather encouraging. She found that she had an overall K2 rating of *favorable/strong* as a tennis coach, but one of *strong/very strong* as a soccer coach. This was not so much because she was any better at soccer than tennis coaching, but that the competition was tougher in tennis coaching. There were loads of good tennis coaches around, but not so many good soccer coaches.

In tennis coaching, the most important K2s were a good standard of tennis playing, a personable character and communication skills. Against all of these Cheryl rated well, but no better than many of her peers. A couple of clients remarked that they thought Cheryl was great, but so too was her boss at the Pines, George, and so too was the whole tennis coaching team at the Cheyenne Mountain Country Club. "The management there demands excellence, nothing short. If the coaches weren't top notch, they'd be booted out on their backsides," said one client.

In soccer coaching, it was a different story. The Palmer Pumas Under 16s were a group of girls who had been playing together for a number of years, some of them since they were in the Under 9s. They had seen coaches come and go. The girls also had siblings who had been in different teams, some with great coaches, some not so lucky. Most of the coaches had good soccer skills, but too many just didn't have the right people skills to coach kids.

Some coaches were unpunctual, showing up late. Some had bullying tendencies, belittling kids when they made mistakes. Some were primadonnas, sadly keen to impress the kids with their dribbling prowess. And some simply couldn't control the group without shouting, swearing and resorting to punishment—making both the mischievous and the earnest but error-prone run round the pitch, again and again.

Other coaches were brilliant. They encouraged the kids, motivated them and looked like they were enjoying the sessions as much as the kids were. They controlled the kids through communicating a sense of corporate responsibility to their team-mates. One such coach, six out of seven of her respondents said, was Cheryl. The seventh was less laudatory, perhaps still smarting after Cheryl had substituted her daughter at half time the previous weekend!

One dad gushed: "Cheryl, you're a gem!"

Following this feedback, Cheryl rated herself as *favorable* on soccer skills, *very strong* on character, *very strong* on communication skills, and *strong* on group control. Overall, she gave herself a K2 rating of *strong/very strong* against a peer group rather less impressive than in tennis coaching.

Cheryl discussed these findings with Chuck. He was delighted. He was unconcerned at her lower K2 rating in tennis coaching; he saw no problem with being a *favorable/strong* performer in a marketplace with tough competition. And he was greatly impressed with her K2 rating in soccer coaching.

But the future was a different matter. For her proposed new venture, Kickabout, to be a success, Cheryl not only had to be an excellent soccer coach. She had to be a good marketer and a good manager. And what training or experience did she have for that? None!

Chuck asked Cheryl to look into some

alternatives for how she could get some basic training in management skills under her belt.

Debi's K2 Rating

It was a cinch for Debi to rate her performance as a receptionist. She'd had so many reviews over the years from various bosses she was all too aware of her strengths and weaknesses in the job.

Against the two most important K2s, personality/attitude and communication skills, Debi didn't hesitate to give herself a rating of *very strong.* And she'd challenge anyone to dispute that! Organizational skills were a different matter. There's no doubt she had improved, she'd had to, after one trying performance review a couple of years back, where her boss had tendered the phrase "charmingly scatty." But the best she could rate herself there was *favorable,* and she couldn't honestly give herself even that for time management. Timekeeping just wasn't Debi's forte, so she'd have to make do with an *okay-ish.*

Overall, taking into account the relative importance of each K2, she rated herself *strong* in the marketplace for reception services.

The K2s for a marketing assistant had a different emphasis, as Debi had found in the previous chapter. Less on the personality and communications side of things, more on the organizational side. Then there was a new K2 of marketing training, of which she'd had none, so she supposed she would have to rate herself as *weak* there.

With a *favorable* and a *weak* on the two most important K2s, and an *okay-ish* and two *very strongs* on the other important K2s, Debi figured that overall she could probably scrape a *favorable* rating in this market. She wondered if that would be good enough for Chuck.

Chuck was mildly encouraged. But he wanted Debi to go away and come back with the answers to two questions: what further steps should she take to improve her organizational skills, and what training could she undertake to learn more about marketing. Debi set off to find out.

In Short

How do you rate against each K2 in your marketplace? And overall?

How does that compare with your main competitors?

How may your rating improve over the next few years?

Any chance you won't get past first base? Is it your attitude?

7 Will You Make Your Plan?

I am a slow walker, but I never walk backwards.
—Abraham Lincoln

In Chapter 1 you were asked to think about your plans over the next few years. For many readers, plans will be nonexistent. If pressed you'll say that you expect to be doing more or less what you're doing now—but hopefully with a pay raise or two.

That's fine. We'll assume that your "plan" is a steady improvement on what it is today. You can review that "plan" in just the same way as you can a rigorously prepared business plan.

Many readers will have general plans, such as switching the balance of their work from one business chunk into another. Like Debi, who wants to move away from reception work and more into marketing.

Other readers will have more specific plans, for example, to venture into a new area—a new service, or a new customer group. Like Cheryl, who has plans to start a new kids' soccer venture.

How Achievable Is Your Plan?

The key to whether your planned revenues (or pay, if you're an employee) are reasonable is *consistency* within a market context. You need to ensure that your plans for the future are consistent with these two main areas of evidence:

- Market demand prospects (as in Chapter 2)
- Your K2 rating, now and over the next few years (as in Chapter 6)

These supplementary areas of evidence may also have a bearing:

- The nature of competition over the next few years (as in Chapter 3)
- Your recent track record: your revenue or pay growth over the last couple of years in relation to growth in market demand over the same period (if you're self-employed) or in relation to fellow employees (if you're an employee).

Here's an example of consistency: If you find that market demand is set to grow steadily, and you assess yourself as having a favorable K2 rating, then all else being equal, you should be able to grow your business at the same pace as the market.

"All else being equal" may well include (a) your finding that the market isn't likely to become more competitive, and (b) the fact that you have a track record in recent years of being able to grow your business along with the market. If your plan over the next few years is simply to grow your business at the same pace as the market, then your backer should find it achievable. If, however, your plan is to grow way faster than that, he'll need much convincing.

Your backer won't necessarily be fazed by a high growth plan, as long as it's consistent. Suppose your K2 rating in a business chunk has been and should remain *strong*, and is demonstrated by your having outperformed the market in the past. If you're planning to continue to beat the market in the future, then your backer should find the assumptions consistent.

But suppose your K2 rating is just *okay-ish* and you've underperformed against the market in the past. And suppose that your K2 rating isn't expected to improve in the future. If your plans show you *beating* the market in the future, your backer's eyebrows will be raised. Your plans are *inconsistent* with both your future K2 rating and your previous performance.

Suppose, however, you've underperformed against the market in the past, but you've recently taken steps to improve your K2 rating to *favorable*. If you're planning to grow with the market in the future, then your story will at least be consistent. But your backer will need to confirm that you have indeed sharpened up your act.

Don't Forget the "Bottom-Up" Approach

The above market-driven, "top-down" approach offers a first cut at assessing achievability, no more. It assumes that you will be continuing to offer the *same* range of services to the *same* customer groups in the future as you did in the past. This may not be so. You may have *specific initiatives* up your sleeve to justify your planned earnings.

These represent breaks with the past. You may be set to broaden, or conversely to narrow, the precise mix of services you offer. Likewise you may be set to broaden (or narrow) your range of customers.

This applies as much to employees as to the self-employed. Our employee exemplar, Debi, is planning to shift from reception to marketing services. Likewise, our sports coach, Cheryl, is planning to add a soccer coaching new venture to her tennis coaching activities.

For the self-employed, your bottom-up initiatives may include significant changes to your cost structure. If this is so, assessing revenue prospects within a market context will only give you part of the answer. Assessing profit plans, taking into account market competition and pricing, will give you some more. But the final answer may depend on the feasibility of your bottom-up investment or cost saving initiatives. This is set out in detail in the big sister version of this book, *Backing U!*

Are Cheryl's Plans Achievable?

Chuck Cash has already found what he needs to know on the markets Cheryl operates in (Chapters 2 and 3) and how well placed she is in those markets (Chapter 6). He's ready to assess whether her plans seem realistic.

Sputnik

In June 2004, a 17-year-old Siberian tennis player became the lowest seeded player ever to become Wimbledon Ladies champion. Yet her victory had been ten years in the making. When just seven years old, she left her mother behind in Russia to enroll in a Florida tennis academy. Her father washed dishes to support her. If you had backed her in the late 1990s, your business plan may have projected solid earnings from a career on the WTA tour. But it would not have anticipated such an early win in a major. Nor that her tournament earnings (now well over $10 million) would be dwarfed by those from commercial endorsements, which have feasted on her athletic and aesthetic image. Her earnings have lifted off the chart.

He finds that they're a bit challenging. They're more likely not to happen than to happen. But they're not too far out.

Chuck has no problem with Cheryl's forecasts for her continuing businesses—coaching tennis at the Pines, at CSSU, and at the two elementary schools. Market demand prospects seem healthy and Cheryl has a *favorable/strong* K2 rating. She has assumed no change in hours coached per week and a fee increase at the Pines of just a few bucks an hour over a three-year period, from $45/hour to $48. This all seems reasonable.

But Chuck suspects there's an air of optimism about the Kickabout forecasts. Cheryl will be giving up secure revenues of $6,500 a year from the Palmer Pumas, to be replaced by Kickabout generating an operating profit of $33,000. Overall, Cheryl is forecasting her operating profit to rise from $51,100 to $77,600, an increase of 52 percent.

Chuck agrees with Cheryl that Kickabout *could* generate profits at that level. But that's not the *most likely* level. Cheryl's forecasts of the numbers of kids and coaches seem reasonable, likewise the costs of park hire, footballs, goals, marketing and admin, but she may have been optimistic in three areas:

- Cheryl believes that parents will be prepared to pay $12 per kid per 45 minute training session, the same as charged by the similar club in Denver. Chuck wonders whether Cheryl will get the initial take-up rates she's hoping for at that fee level and thinks $10 would be more realistic for the first year or two, perhaps scaling up to $12 by year three or four.

- Cheryl thinks she can get her target take-up rates (12 paying kids per group, 12 groups, over a three-hour period on a Saturday morning) after one year of operations. Perhaps, but it would be safer to assume that she reaches those levels only by year three or four.

- Cheryl assumes that she needs just herself plus one other experienced coach to supervise a couple of less experienced coaches plus four student coaches. Chuck suspects this may be unrealistic for a startup and that punters will expect four experienced coaches (Cheryl included), pushing the average fee for a subcontracted coach up from Cheryl's assumed $32 per hour to $35.

Chuck's more conservative assumptions lower Kickabout's forecast operating profit from $33,000 to $20,100 in year 3. But this still increases Cheryl's income to $64,600, 27 percent up from what she's earning today.

And Chuck likes the business. He's impressed at how Cheryl has spotted a niche market opportunity and worked up a sound business proposition.

She's looking backable. But what risks does this venture hold, Chuck wonders. That's for the next chapter.

Are Debi's Plans Achievable?

Chuck doesn't have a problem with Debi's forecasts. Market demand for reception services in New York is likely to contract, and competition among receptionists to heat up, but Little, Stamp's prospects seem sound and Debi's K2 rating *strong*. Debi has had pay raises of 2 to 3 percent a year over the last few years, taking her to $35,538, plus an annual bonus of up to $1,650. She is forecasting similar pay raises over the next three years, and this does not seem unreasonable.

But Chuck has a slight problem with where Debi believes she will derive her earnings. She anticipates being able to transfer within Little, Stamp to a role whereby she would work 50 percent at reception, 50 percent with the marketing department.

If Debi were self-employed, an independent contractor to Little, Stamp, Chuck wonders whether these numbers would stack up. Sure Debi should achieve her $19,000 revenue target in year three from reception services, but would she achieve the same amount from marketing services, given a K2 rating barely bordering on *favorable?*

Chuck figures he'll have to look closely at the risks involved for Debi in making this role transfer within the company. Would she not be safer as a receptionist who can occasionally do marketing work, as opposed to someone who is officially allocated half-time to reception, half-time to marketing? That's for Chapter 8.

In Short

Are your earnings plans consistent—especially with market demand forecasts and your K2 rating?

Do they reflect any bottom-up initiatives you are planning?

Are your plans achievable?

8 How Risky?

When written in Chinese the word crisis is composed of two characters. One represents danger, and the other represents opportunity.—John F. Kennedy

In the last chapter, you assessed whether your plans are likely to work out. You're almost there, but for one final stage. How risky are U? How likely is it that one or two or the risks you've met along the way will blow your plans? Conversely, what are the odds of one or two of those opportunities enabling you to beat your plans?

Gather Together the Main Risks and Opportunities

This is where you need to cast a fresh eye over the work you've already done in earlier chapters, especially Chapters 2, 3, 6, and 7, and pull out the main risks and opportunities you've uncovered.

When you forecast market demand in Chapter 2, what did you identify as the main risks of those forecasts not being met? Conversely, did you come across any opportunities that could cause those forecasts to be exceeded?

And what about competition risks and

opportunities in Chapter 3? Or those relating to your K2 rating in Chapter 6? And to your plan in Chapter 7?

By now you should have identified a half-dozen or so risks and the same number of opportunities. Only go for the main ones. There's no need to pull out every eventuality.

Look for Big Risks and Opportunities

Now you need to gauge which of these risks and opportunities *really* matter. As opposed to those that just matter.

Go through each one and assess how likely it is to happen. Is the likelihood *low, medium,* or *high?* Or somewhere in between, like *low/medium?*

And while you're thinking on that risk or opportunity, assess how big an impact it would make on your future earnings if it did happen. Would the impact be *low, medium,* or *high?*

Now pull out any risk or opportunity that is either of:

- Medium likelihood and high impact
- High likelihood and medium impact
- High likelihood and high impact

These are the risks and opportunities that really matter. These are the "big" risks and opportunities.

Weigh Up the Big Risks and Opportunities

Now you've pinpointed the big risks and opportunities, you need to ask yourself two questions: Is there a showstopper risk? And do the opportunities, on balance, outshine the risks?

A showstopper risk is one that is both very likely *and* very big. If your backer finds one of them in your business or job, then that's it. You're unbackable in your current job or business.

Conversely, you may find an *opportunity* that is both very likely *and* very big. That's a big, maybe mega opportunity, and your backer will be falling over himself to invest in you.

Some risks are huge, but most unlikely to happen. That's not to say that they might not happen. The unlikely sometimes happens. But if we worried about the unlikely happening we would never cross the road. Certainly no backer would ever invest a cent!

The second question you need to address is this: Do the big opportunities outshine the big risks? If so, then you may well be backable in your current business or job.

Or is it the other way round? Do the big risks outweigh the big opportunities? Then you may not be backable.

Could Your Attitude Blow Your Plans?

There's one check we must make before leaving this chapter. Is there any chance that your attitude is a showstopper risk? Could it become so?

Suppose you're in a job where your attitude is not great but it's unlikely to cost you your job. You assess your attitude risk as of low likelihood, high impact. But change is on the way. A new boss is due to take over, and she sees things in a different light. She wants to put customer service top priority, with attitude a must-have K2 for all her team. Your attitude could become a showstopper risk.

How Risky Is Cheryl?

Chuck is impressed with Cheryl. He likes the markets she's in, admires how she excels in her coaching jobs, and is excited by the new business opportunity she has spotted. And he likes her as a person, as does everyone who meets her. But he's a pro investor. He mustn't get carried away. He sits down and considers the risks he'll be taking on if he backs her. He combs through his analysis of earlier chapters and pulls out five main risks:

1. The current popularity of tennis turns out to be a fad, replaced by some other sport or activity, maybe cricket or Tai-Chi (from Chapter 2).
2. Kickabout takes off and does well, but someone, possibly one of Cheryl's subcontracted coaches, starts up a rival venture (Chapter 3).
3. Cheryl's subcontracted coaches demand more of the action if Kickabout succeeds (Chapter 3).
4. Cheryl has no experience in managing and marketing an organization (Chapter 6).
5. Cheryl's business plan was rather optimistic, indicating some naiveté in financial planning (Chapter 7).

Chuck weighs these risks carefully. The first is of low likelihood, though potentially

Pay Her for Win

Back in 1983, a young woman applied for a job to host WLS-TV's low-rated, half-hour, morning talk show, *AM Chicago*. Successful talk shows at the time were hosted by white, middle-class males, many with years of experience in journalism and/or TV reporting. Interviewing skills were seen as integral to the talk show format. This woman was black, female, working class, and overweight. And her experience was in presenting, not reporting. Those were five *big* risks, each with high likelihood, high impact. Would you have backed her that day? Perhaps you too would have spotted the extraordinary personality—the articulacy, empathy, and vitality. Her personality was *the* big opportunity, which surpassed the big risks. O happy day.

high impact, while the third is more likely, but of lower impact. So they're not "big" risks. The fifth he discounts—he can help Cheryl with financial planning, and the two of them have already agreed Chuck's downgraded forecasts for Kickabout.

Only risks 2 and 4 are big ones. Number 2 is likely only if Kickabout proves a great success, which is fine, as long as the copycat entrepreneur does his sums right and stimulates enough demand for both businesses to thrive. Number 4 is medium/high in both likelihood and impact, but it's a risk Cheryl can do something about. She can take evening classes in business management and marketing, and Chuck can help her relate what she learns to the real world as she goes along.

Meanwhile Chuck has also found three main opportunities:

1. Americans continue to seek greater fitness and health, and one such route could remain playing tennis, and especially for their children, soccer (Chapter 2).

2. A Kickabout lookalike has been successful in Denver and should be replicable in Colorado Springs (Chapters 2 and 3).

3. If Kickabout draws in the numbers of kids Cheryl believes it will, she may be able to nudge up prices after a few years and make a healthy operating margin (Chapter 7).

Opportunity 1 is the counterbalance to risk 1, and Chuck believes, more credible. But it is opportunities 2 and 3 Chuck really likes. They are both medium/high in both likelihood and impact. In other words, they are "big" opportunities.

To Chuck, these two big opportunities clearly surpass the two big risks. Cheryl is looking backable. But before he gives the go ahead, he needs to put the whole storyline in context. That's for the next chapter.

How Risky Is Debi?

Chuck had already figured out what the biggest risk in backing Debi was: She was in danger of becoming neither one thing nor another. She didn't yet have the capabilities to succeed in marketing, but she was keen to move across from reception, where she was exceptionally capable.

Chuck was his customary rigorous self, however, and gathered together all the main risks and opportunities. He found six main risks:

1. The New York financial crisis leads to economic depression, not just recession, and to intense competition for office work (Chapters 2 and 3).
2. Security staff take over reception duties (Chapters 2 and 3).
3. New York publishers lose out to lower cost rivals (Chapters 2 and 3).
4. Debi's organizational shortcomings for a marketing role (Chapter 6).
5. Debi's lack of marketing training (Chapter 6).
6. Debi neglects reception work in favor of marketing work (Chapter 7).

Of these risks, the first three were either of low likelihood (numbers 1 and 3) or of low impact (number 2), so they weren't "big" risks. Risks 4 and 5 were bigger, but one at least could be mitigated. Debi's lack of marketing training could be addressed either at the office or outside, at evening classes. Debi had already identified an appropriate course, and subject to Chuck's approval, she'll enroll immediately. As for Debi's organizational deficiencies, she will have to resolve to address them.

The big risk remained the last one—that Debi might so neglect her receptionist role in focusing on her marketing role that she gets replaced by a new receptionist and then doesn't make the grade as a marketing assistant. But again, this risk was within Debi's power to control (and Chuck's, if he backs her).

Chuck found three main opportunities before Debi:

1. Good growth prospects for Little, Stamp, especially in self-help books (Chapter 2).
2. Debi's personality and communication skills, for both reception and marketing work (Chapter 6).
3. Debi's enthusiasm for taking on a greater marketing role (Chapter 6).

These were all "big" opportunities. A growing Little, Stamp meant jobs at the firm would continue to be created, rather than cut back— so high likelihood, medium impact. Debi's personality and communication skills meant that a reception job at least was there for the keeping. And her enthusiasm for taking on more of a marketing role boded well for her motivation in addressing some of her weaknesses.

The opportunities seemed to outshine the risks, especially since the one really big risk was largely within Debi's power to control. Debi was looking backable.

In Short

What main risks and opportunities did you find in earlier chapters?

Which were "big"? Did you find a showstopper risk?

Do the big opportunities outshine the big risks?

How's your attitude? Is it a big risk?

9 Would You Back U?

In the last chapter you assessed whether the risks around achieving your business plan were surpassed by the opportunities of exceeding them. You're all but ready to conclude whether you're backable in your current job or business. All that's needed now is a simple storyline to underpin and justify your conclusion.

This is the fun bit. All—yes, *all*—the hard work has already been done. What you need to do now is extract the conclusions from each of Chapters 2, 3, 6, 7, and 8, and weave them into a coherent storyline. One that puts the backing decision in full context.

And that storyline will lead you to answer the key question behind Part I of this book: *Would you back U in your current business or job?*

Developing the Storyline

What you need to aim for is a series of conclusions, which when put together suggest an *overall* conclusion, the answer to the key question above.

You should set the storyline out as follows. The overall conclusion on why you are or aren't backable (in which you summarize the main findings from the headlines below):

- *Market demand prospects*—Your conclusions on what's going to happen to market demand (Chapter 2).
- *Competition*—Your conclusions on whether competition is tough and going to get tougher (Chapter 3).
- *Your K2 rating*—Your conclusions on how you stack up against the competition, now and over the next few years (Chapter 6).
- *Your plan*—Your conclusions on whether your plans are achievable (Chapter 7).
- *Risks and opportunities*—Your conclusions on the main risks and opportunities that may affect your plan (Chapter 8).

This storyline must be concise. You must force yourself to get right to the point. Each bullet point should be no more than one sentence. It can have a couple of commas, with some backup qualifying phrases, maybe even a dash or a colon. But just the one sentence.

The more long-winded you make this storyline, the more difficult it will be to derive your overall conclusion, the answer in the overall headline. The answer itself, to the key question *Would you back U?,* should also be just the one, conclusive sentence.

What's Your Storyline?

What's your storyline? It may not be pretty. The fact that you're reading this book means that you may harbor some doubts on your backability.

Try to be totally objective and dispassionate. Think what Chuck would conclude. *Not what you'd want him to conclude.* Develop a fair and balanced storyline, but make sure it's independent, hard-hitting, and conclusive.

Would You Back U in Your Current Business or Job?

Once you've developed your storyline, that's almost it. Would you back U in your current business or job? *Yes,* or *no.* Or perhaps, *yes, if...* Or even, *no, but...*

If the answer has a *yes* in it, you should find Part II helpful. This shows how to set about performing even better in your current business or job.

If, however, the answer includes a *no,* please turn to Part III. You need to find a business or job where you stand a better chance of succeeding. Part III will show you how to find a career where you aspire to be, a career that inspires you.

It will show you how to back the passion in you.

Would You Back Cheryl?

Let's look at the storyline Chuck has drawn up on Cheryl:

Cheryl seems well placed in a thriving sports coaching market in Colorado Springs and the opportunity for her new venture, Kickabout, to succeed outshines copycat and managerial risks:

- *Market demand prospects*—Demand for both tennis and soccer coaching seems set to grow further in Colorado Springs, driven by popular concern for a fitter, healthier lifestyle, while there may be a gap in the market for the Kickabout concept.
- *Competition*—Competition in Colorado Springs sports coaching is moderately tough, with more providers and lower entry barriers in soccer than tennis, while direct competition to Kickabout seems unlikely in the short-term.
- *Cheryl's K2 rating*—Cheryl seems favorably placed against strong competition in tennis coaching, and strongly placed against variable competition in soccer coaching, but she'll need new marketing and management skills for Kickabout.
- *Cheryl's plan*—Cheryl's profit forecasts for Kickabout seem optimistic, but she could nevertheless boost her earnings by one third over three years.
- *Risks and opportunities*—The opportunity for Kickabout to succeed surpasses the risks of a copycat startup and Cheryl's lack of management experience.

Will Chuck back Cheryl? The answer

Stone Un-Broke

In 1992, a then little-known Hollywood actress was cast for a leading role in a big-budget movie. Many of Hollywood's leading ladies had turned down the role, perhaps because of the risqué, occasionally violent sex scenes. You were thinking of backing her. These may have been your conclusions:

She seems set to shine in what could well be a high-grossing movie, enhancing her Hollywood marketability and enabling her to meet, even exceed, her plans:

- *Market demand prospects*—Demand for lead female actresses in Hollywood thrillers is buoyant, although hits in the steamy, femme fatale, *Body Heat* genre are infrequent.

- *Competition*—Competition for lead female roles gets stiffer each year but has been limited for this movie, with many stars turned off by its explicitness.

- *Her K2 rating*—Her career has been patchy, with forays into B movies, but this movie could make her highly marketable—her producers say her auditions were sensational, conveying smoldering sensuality and *sang froid*.

- *Her plan*—Her financial plans should be met if she acts on a par with her co-star, and greatly exceeded if the movie is a box office hit.

- *Risks and opportunities*—The opportunity for this movie to be a hit, with its blend of intrigue, lust, and Californian splendor, seems to outshine the risk of it flopping because of her current lack of star pull.

Would you have backed her? Would you have trusted your basic instinct?

must surely be yes. He will require her to undertake some management and marketing training, but he'll back her. Would you? Your investment wouldn't be without risk, but no investment ever is.

Would You Back Debi?

Here's Chuck's storyline on Debi:

Debi seems well placed at Little, Stamp and should continue to shine there, as long as she plays to her strengths in reception work while steadily building her capabilities in marketing:

- *Market demand prospects*—New York market demand for reception and marketing services seems set to contract short-term with recession, while demand within successful publishers like Little, Stamp should hold firm.
- *Competition*—Competition will intensify short-term for jobs in reception and marketing services, both with low entry barriers and attractive to applicants of medium levels of educational achievement, but should ease with resumed growth medium-term.
- *Debi's K2 rating*—Debi is strongly placed as a receptionist, and favorably placed as a marketing assistant, where she would benefit from sharpening up her organizational skills and from training.
- *Debi's plan*—Debi's financial targets

are sensible, but her assumption that these can be achieved through working half-time in the Marketing Department may be challenging.

- *Risks and opportunities*— Opportunities at Little, Stamp and in Debi's personality and enthusiasm seem to outshine the main risk of Debi neglecting reception work to focus on marketing.

Will Chuck back Debi? The answer seems like a yes, or a qualified yes. He will back her as long as she guarantees that she will remain committed to her main job as a receptionist and not apply for an official part-time job in marketing within the next couple of years. By then she should have more experience and some marketing training under her belt. And hopefully performance reviews will show that her organizational skills have improved. Only then will he consider backing a firm commitment to marketing work.

In essence, his advice to Debi would be what he has advised scores of clients over the years: "Debs, by all means aim for the work you really want, but take care you hold on to a fallback position. Be prepared for things not to work out as hoped. Don't burn your bridges!"

In Short

What's your storyline?

Would you back U in your current job or business?

Part II

Becoming More Backable

Introduction

All that is human must retrograde if it does not advance.—Edward Gibbon

Part II is for you if you concluded in Part I that you would back U in your current job or business. Your earnings target is likely to be met. Opportunities seem to outshine the risks in your current field.

If you were dissatisfied with your job before reading Part I, perhaps you are a trifle less so now? Were you perhaps suffering from the human trait of seeing the grass as greener on the other side? Has the grass on your own side started to get a shade or two greener? I hope so.

Part II builds on the work you have already carried out in Part I. It shows you how to improve your prospects in your current field, shortening the odds on success, making yourself more backable.

We start with some brainstorming.

Nothing is harder on your laurels than resting on them.—Anonymous

10 Envision the Capabilities of the Ideal Provider

The man who has no imagination has no wings.
—Muhammad Ali

The first step in making yourself more back-able is to envision the future of the marketplace in which you work. Will it be more competitive? Will customers have different expectations? Will providers need to develop different capabilities?

To do this, it helps if you can do some brainstorming. Brainstorming may conjure up images of smart, flashy yuppies pacing around the conference room table fixing yellow stickies to flipcharts, while nibbling on their Brazil nuts and dried apricots and sipping Perrier. Perhaps—and fine if that's you—but there are plenty of other ways of brainstorming.

What you do need to do is try to think a bit more creatively and laterally than you may have done in Chapters 2 through 4. You need to go through and beyond those chapters. Get the right-hand side of the brain working.

Different folks have different strokes for thinking laterally. Some think most creatively in bed, some in front of a log fire, others in a place of worship. Some meditate, some do yoga, others soak in a flotation tank. Me? I walk. The setting has to be green, preferably with plenty of blue. The cliff paths of the West Wales coastline are perfect, with fields, hedgerows, and baaing sheep to one side, the Cambrian Sea, rocks and squawking cormorants to the other. If I can't be there, a park or golf course will have to do, preferably with a lake or pond and some wildfowl waddling around.

Wherever and however you do it, you need to stimulate those gray cells to think creatively. Try to brainstorm a range of scenarios on what may happen in your marketplace. Venture beyond the more likely outcomes—you've already drawn those up. Think of those that are less expected but still *quite* likely to occur. Stay clear of fanciful outcomes with only a remote chance of happening. Go for scenarios that *could* actually happen. Apply the reasonability test: "Is it reasonable for me to assume that such and such an outcome could take place over the next five years? Sure it may be less likely to happen than other outcomes, but looking back five years from now would I be surprised that it actually happened?"

One or two of your chosen scenarios you'll lift from Chapter 8. This is inevitable. There you pulled together all the main risks and opportunities you had identified in the preceding chapters. Some of them, whether for good or bad, could readily be developed into scenarios.

Other scenarios, especially perhaps on the

opportunity side, may be new. They should hopefully reflect the "out of the box" nature of your brainstorming. They may serve to steer you in a new and promising direction.

Settle on two to four scenarios. Not too many, just a few. Give each a name, something that brings the scenario to life. It will give credibility to the set-up and help you prepare to address it.

If you're an employee, you should follow the same brainstorming process as for the self-employed. But remember that you need to do the thinking at two different levels, just as in Part I. Where might market demand (or competition or customer needs) for your type of services be heading *in general,* and more specifically, where might demand for your type of services be heading *within your company?*

You already had a go at assessing the Key Kapabilities (K2s) required for service providers in your marketplace—see Chapter 5. To what extent will these K2s change under each of the scenarios? Some K2s may become more or less important. Some may be brand new.

Are there any new—or reassessed—K2s that are common to each of the scenarios? What will the *ideal* provider in your market-place look like in three to five years' time? Against which K2s will he or she excel? How will that differ from the ideal provider of today? More qualified? In what? Better trained? In what way? More experienced? In which areas? More skillful? In what?

Cheryl's Envisioning

Having agreed to back Cheryl, Chuck advises her to build on the work they did together in Part I of this book. She can redeploy all that research and analysis to make herself even more backable.

Cheryl's a sportswoman and a sports coach. Some people relax best on a golf course. Not Cheryl; she'd be concentrating too hard on how to groove her swing. For her to relax, it has to be something well away from sport. It will have to be a Thai traditional massage, where her muscles will be probed and ground and her limbs twisted and stretched mercilessly. Then she can think.

Her body still aching from the massage, Cheryl stretches out in her candlelit bath, glass of wine to hand, and envisions the future. She lets her mind float freely between issues of market demand, competition, and customer needs, and comes up with three scenarios, each memorably named:

- *Multi-Media!* Online tennis instruction via video-clip becomes more popular.
- *Kicked!* Her best coach sets up a rival to Kickabout.
- *Clubbing!* Parents come to expect more than just soccer training on a Saturday morning from an organization like Kickabout.

The third scenario, Clubbing!, excites Cheryl. Suppose parents come to demand something more than informal training on a Saturday morning? Suppose they want her to arrange matches against other teams? Or to arrange outings to watch pro soccer games, or even take a trip to the bowling alley? In other words, suppose they expect Kickabout to develop as a club? It seems reasonably likely to happen in the next couple of years. And if it does, Cheryl might have to do something about it.

So what of the ideal provider under these scenarios? Cheryl figures she might need these K2s *over and above* those set out in Chapter 5:

- *Multi-Media!* Technology skills to record players' strokes, download onto a PC, edit the clips with highlights and compare with professionals' strokes.
- *Kicked!* Management and motivational skills to include knowing when and to what extent she should offer a potentially rival coach a share in the revenues or ownership of Kickabout.
- *Clubbing!* Organizational skills (and time) to set up matches and club outings.

Cheryl explores whether any of these extra capabilities are common to all scenarios. There's modest overlap between the management skills required for the Kicked! scenario and the organizational skills required for Clubbing!, but they are more similar to the general management and marketing skills identified as K2s in Chapter 5. Cheryl suspects she should give them even greater emphasis in her plans.

Debi's Envisioning

Let's see how successful our receptionist-cum-marketer, Debi, is with her brainstorming. She, unlike Cheryl, is wholly un-sporty. Her main exercise when younger was dancing the night away at Manhattan's grooviest clubs. These days, as a working mom, she gets all the exercise she needs, and more, thank you, just keeping work, home, and school duties functioning. Ideal relaxation for her comes at the Queens Wellness Centre with an hour's gentle aromatherapy, followed by an hour in the flotation tank. Bliss!

The pampering seems to do the trick and Debi comes up with two scenarios, both more on the risk than the opportunity side:

- *Replaced!* Little, Stamp managers decide they need more cover at reception than they can get from Debi's half-time presence and recruit someone new, leaving Debi reliant on her marketing role to hold her place in the firm.

- *Elbowed!* Another employee at Little, Stamp follows Debi's lead and starts to help out at marketing, offering superior organizational skills than Debi could ever possess.

The first of these scenarios, Replaced!, is related to the main risk Chuck was concerned about, that Debi neglects reception work in favor of marketing work. But this scenario has a different angle. This is not her bosses deciding she isn't motivated enough to continue as a receptionist, but that they need a full-time person for optimal reception cover. Given the firm's recent expansion, this could well happen within a year or two.

The Elbowed! scenario wasn't factored into Chuck's analysis. Indeed, Debi didn't mention to Chuck that one of her colleagues, a PA named Christina, had also helped out at a couple of marketing events and had floated the idea to Debi. If Christina did decide to pursue this interest, she would be formidable competition. Personable, attractive, and according to her colleagues, amazingly efficient, though a touch shy, Debi would be up against it.

Debi meanwhile believes that the ideal provider under her two scenarios will require these capabilities over and above those set out in Chapter 5:

- *Replaced!* There's not much Debi can do about this, whatever skills she possesses. If the firm wants a full-time role, she'll have to make up her mind at the time; until then, all she can hope to do is keep lines of communication open, be flexible, and try to keep both reception and marketing managers happy.
- *Elbowed!* More attention to organizational skills, and perhaps, the development of special communication skills to give an edge over potential challengers for the position.

The only commonality Debi sees between

the extra capabilities required under each of her two scenarios was in communications skills. This, of course, was a K2 already identified in Chapter 5 of being of high importance for reception work and medium in marketing work. Is there some way Debi can maneuver a greater importance for this K2 in the type of marketing work she does? This gives Debi food for thought as she sets out to ponder her objectives in Chapter 11.

In Short

What scenarios can you envision for your marketplace?

What extra K2s will be needed? Are any common to each scenario?

What will the ideal provider look like?

11 Stretch Your Sights and Identify the Capability Gap

Achievement is largely the product of steadily raising one's levels of aspiration...and expectation.
—Jack Nicklaus

Where do you want to be in your current job or business in three, five years' time? What's your vision of yourself? Do you envision being more or less where you are today, doing more or less the same things, serving more or less the same customers?

If the answer is a yes, or a rather less committal "I suppose so," that's fine. You're backable anyway. That's why you're reading Part II of this book.

If, however, you're of a more ambitious nature, you may want to raise those sights. Sure, you're backable now, but how about becoming *more* backable? How about raising the bar on your potential achievements? How about raising the return on your investment in yourself?

That's just one side of the coin, I know. The other side is the nonmonetary, which may be more important to you. Especially if your financial circumstances seem reasonably under control. Caring for or helping other people may be your main driver for job satisfaction, letting the money side of things go hang. That's fine and admirable—as long as the bills get paid.

However you take these nonmonetary factors into account, you may still benefit from coming up with an answer. Where do you want to be in your current job or business in three or five years' time? Do your sights need raising?

There are three main aspects of setting and possibly raising your sights:

1. Which business chunks should you address? The same as now, or others potentially more attractive?
2. What plans do you have to become more competitive and improve your K2 rating?
3. How close to the ideal provider should you aim to become?

Let's clarify what we mean by an attractive business chunk? In the business world, the definition is relatively straightforward. Market attractiveness is often taken to be a blend of four factors: market size, market demand growth, competitive intensity, and market risk.

These factors remain valid for an individual as well. But they're not sufficient. They make no allowance for the soul, for the subjective, something that's often treated as an irrelevance in the corporate world.

We need to add at least a fifth factor, which we can term *enjoyment* (or *fulfillment*, if you prefer). This should give the definition of attractiveness a better balance.

If you're thinking of resetting your sights to address a more attractive business chunk, you should look before you leap. Just do a wee check on why you think the new chunk might be more attractive. Is the market bigger? Growing faster? Less competitive? Lower risk? More fulfilling/enjoyable/stimulating?

Then think about how well placed you would be in that chunk. Are the customer needs (Chapter 4) different? Are different Key Kapabilities needed (Chapter 5)? How would you stack up against your peers (Chapter 6)? Would your K2 rating be better or worse than in your current main business chunk? Would you at least be reasonably placed?

The second main aspect of setting sights concerns your future competitiveness in your main business chunks. What plans do you have to improve your K2 rating over the next few years, as you've already set out in Chapters 6 and 7?

These are your current sights. But should they be stretched? This brings us to the third main aspect: How close to the ideal provider should you aim to become?

Where do you want to be in tomorrow's marketplace? Are your sights currently set on bridging the K2 gap found in Part I? Or should you consider raising your sights toward bridging the likely wider K2 gap of Chapter 10?

Do you want to become a good player in tomorrow's marketplace? A strong player?

Or do you want to go for goal and *lead* in tomorrow's marketplace? Do you want to get as far as you can toward becoming tomorrow's ideal provider?

Why not? The fact that you're reading this book indicates you're serious about self-development. Why not stretch your sights the whole way and go for goal in tomorrow's market?

You can now identify the K2 gap. You've revisited your K2 ratings from Chapter 6, compared them with those of the ideal provider and set your sights on the extent you wish to bridge the gap. That's your target K2 gap. In the next chapter, you'll develop a strategy on how to bridge it.

Cheryl's Sights and K2 Gap

First things first, thinks Cheryl. Tennis coaching will still account for 70 percent of earnings going forward (under Chuck's amended forecasts), even if Kickabout is successful. So if she's to do any raising of sights, she'd better think about tennis first, soccer second.

The Multi-Media! scenario doesn't particularly worry her. Video instruction is already offered at The Cheyenne Mountain Country Club, a main competitor to the Pines, but only one or two of Cheryl's clients have ever asked for it. But what if Cheryl raises her sights? Suppose she learns not just how to switch on the DVD camcorder but to edit the video clip too? That would both make her stand out from the competition and protect her should the Multi-Media scenario take off. The trouble is that Cheryl verges on the technophobe. Maybe she'll just have to bite the bullet and leapfrog from the stone to the virtual age in one bound.

The other two scenarios, Kicked! and Clubbed!, relate to her new soccer venture, Kickabout. Cheryl can prepare herself for these scenarios through further training in management and marketing, which she could do at a local college. But what if she raises her sights, goes for goal (literally!), and enrolls on a part-time MBA program at CSSU?

In summary, Cheryl identifies her target K2 gap as follows:

- Management skills—running a small company, motivating employees
- Marketing skills—promoting a new venture cost-effectively
- Organizational skills—administering, perhaps through delegation, the potential transition of Kickabout from a training group to a club
- Technology skills—learning how to edit video clips on a PC

Next she needs a strategy on how to bridge this K2 gap over the next few years...

Debi's Sights and K2 Gap

Debi already found (in Chapter 6) a considerable K2 gap between her and the ideal provider of marketing services at Little, Stamp. Chuck advised that she needed to sharpen her organizational skills and undertake some marketing training. In Chapter 10, Debi identified a scenario, Elbowed!, whereby someone with much greater organizational skills might overtake and displace her for a role in marketing.

Debi decides to raise her sights. Her discussions with Chuck had only reinforced her determination to move away from reception work over time. She doesn't want to be still doing reception work in her mid-forties—well, at least not without having given something else a darn good go.

She's going to go for goal. She'll undergo some training in marketing, and also in organizational skills. And she'll unleash her secret weapon, a preemptive strike on the Elbowed! scenario. She's already a terrific communicator around the office. Everyone knows that. But she's had no experience in communicating with an audience. A role in the marketing department will only now and again make available an opportunity to speak to a large gathering, but if she can do it well—or at least better than others in the department, and certainly better than prospective leap-frogger Christina—she'll have an extra and mighty arrow in her quiver.

She's going to become a speaker!

She's not sure how she's going to do this, but she resolves to start looking around at the options. She doesn't know it, but the solution to her problem lies on her doorstep, so inexpensive as to be virtually free and a huge amount of fun to boot. She'll find out what it is in the next chapter.

In Short

What is the K2 gap between you and tomorrow's ideal provider?

What plans did you have to reduce it?

Should you stretch your sights and narrow it further?

12 Select Your Strategy to Bridge the Gap

It is not enough to stare up the steps, we must step up the stairs.—Vaclav Havel

Ask a dozen businesspeople, economists, generals, or politicians how to define strategy and you'll get a dozen different answers. Here's mine: *Strategy is how you deploy your resources to gain a sustainable advantage over the competition.*

You've already assessed what resources, or Key Kapabilities you have. You rated them in Chapter 6. And again in Chapter 11 when you identified your target K2 gap. You're ready to draw up your strategy.

There are three main generic strategies for an individual to achieve his or her goals. The first two are based on generic business strategies. To develop a sustainable competitive advantage, and to enjoy profitable growth, companies generally follow either (1) a differentiation strategy, or (2) a low-cost strategy. To simplify, they either do something distinctive and well, or do more or less the same as the others but at lower cost. What they would be well advised *not* to do is exactly the same as other companies do, the so-called *me-too* recipe for lack of success.

For an individual, whether employed or self-employed, these generic business strategies are directly transferable. Let's call the differentiation strategy the *Stand Out!* strategy, since we can all get a handle on the importance of standing out, being special to someone or some group of people (customers). It's making your offering distinctive, different from the next provider. It's a strategy that builds on your strengths, and circumvents your weaknesses.

For the low-cost strategy, let's call it the *easyU!* strategy. European readers will be familiar with the astonishing success of the low-cost airline easyJet (similar to the success of Southwest Airlines in the United States), which later diversified into a range of other low-cost offerings in other sectors, such as easyCar, easyMoney, and easyMobile. If you're going to make your offering the lowest cost on the market, then easyU! just about sums it up. It's a strategy that aims to maximize your utilization (your average number of *paid* days per week). It's the strategy of the self-employed car mechanic, the immigrant laborer, the aging professional, many a working mom.

But for individuals, there's a third generic strategy that is important. That is where circumstances combine to constrain your pursuit of the other two strategies. You may not be able to differentiate sufficiently, you may not choose to become the lowest cost provider, but you do need to improve your competitiveness, your

K2 rating, or you may find yourself in trouble. We'll call that the *Sharpen Act!* strategy. It's not the optimal, perhaps, but it could well be better than no strategy at all.

In the Sharpen Act! strategy, you build on your strengths to the extent that you're able to in the circumstances, but meanwhile you work on some of the weaknesses that are holding you down. You set out to improve your K2 rating.

Once you've decided on your generic strategy, you need to make a plan. You know where you want to get to. You know how you want to travel there. But which route do you take? The answers are, of course, as many and diverse as getting from your home to the office, from London to Timbuktu, or from Las Vegas to heaven!

There is any number of permutations of investment in time, effort, and cash that could make up your plan. Your challenge is to narrow down the universe of alternatives into those two or three most strategically consistent and viable.

If you're self-employed, there are six main areas you may need to invest in, namely marketing, training, equipment, premises, staff, and partnering. If you're an employee, the latter four are unlikely to be relevant. For employees, investment in training is likely to be the most important, but investment in marketing should not be dismissed. Let's take a look at these two first, since they apply to all of us.

Investment in marketing. There are hundreds of thousands of self-employed people out there, like—I have to admit—me, who just don't devote enough time, effort, and cash to marketing. Then we complain when the phone doesn't ring.

Marketing is the life-blood of the self-employed. But it can be important too for an employee. You're not going to get far being good at your job if no one in your organization knows it.

Investment in training. This is often the key investment option for the employee. There may be areas of training provided by your company. But what if that training doesn't coincide with what you need to bridge your K2 gap? Then you have three choices. You can try to persuade your boss that it is in the company's interests for you to broaden your offering through this training. Or you can leave the company for a similar company where that training will form part of the employment package. Or you can finance it yourself in your spare time—as long you're reasonably confident that it will prove a sound investment.

If you're self-employed, training can be just as important. You may need further training in your field of specialization, or you may need to diversify into a related field. You may need some serious training or coaching in an area of deficiency, for example selling skills. But the opportunity costs of your time could be high, and any cash costs will usually be to your account—unless you can persuade your customers to chip in, as can sometimes be beneficial to both parties.

The self-employed need to consider other areas of investment.

Investment in equipment or premises. The key is to draw up your selection criteria carefully—especially your investment cost limits.

Unlike a Virgin

A young girl of Italian descent arrived in New York in 1978 with just a few dollars in her pocket. She struggled gamely for five years before landing a recording contract. She went on to become the most successful female performing artist in history, despite, many would say, possessing limited talent. How? Through a single-minded *Stand Out!* strategy, perhaps thus: To build on capabilities in the performing arts through sustained investment of cash, time, and energy in image reinvention and self-publicity. The material girl has applied this strategy ruthlessly for over 25 years, enabling her to ride through such potentially career-limiting horrors as her venture into eroticism in 1992. Her strategy slotted into the groove.

Screen the options available and narrow down to those that best fit your criteria. Think of buying a house—or even a digital camera. The choice can be daunting at first, but the options soon get whittled down.

Investment in staff. Here, you need to feel comfortable that the extra revenues you'll be able to generate with an employee on board are greater than the total extra costs incurred from engaging the employee—including wages, benefits, social security, insurance, and incremental overhead.

Investment in partnership. Partnerships can be joined to enable a joint investment in premises, equipment, or both. A partnership shares the risk. Many professional practices are partnerships, whether lawyers, doctors, vets, alternative therapists. They reduce financial risk, but they introduce a new area of risk, namely dependence on others. Your partners need to share the same core aims, horizons, and values as you.

You may now have developed two or three strategic alternatives, each representing a defined and coherent strategy for bridging your K2 gap. They may reflect investment in one area alone, or investment in a combination of areas. Alternative A, for example, may involve further training in marketing skills, while alternative B may involve partnership with a proven marketer.

These alternatives need evaluating. The optimal alternative can sometimes be obvious (see Debi's tale), but often investment appraisal is complex. Chuck Cash would say he seeks the alternative that gives him and his client *the highest return for the lowest risk*. But that's not always readily apparent. (If in doubt, flip through this book's big sister, *Backing U!)*

So you've decided on your strategic plan. That's the easy part! What's tricky is carrying it through, in implementing the strategy.

For that you'll need to draw up an action plan. This will be a checklist of all the actions you need to undertake to achieve your strategy, including a start date and a target completion date. Be realistic in the timing. Don't plan for the impossible.

The key to getting things done is to revisit your action plan regularly, say once a month. Chastise yourself if you've fallen behind in one area, thereby impacting another. What are you going to do to ensure such slippage doesn't happen again?

Cheryl's Strategy

Cheryl had done her brainstorming, scenario envisioning, and sketching of the ideal provider. She had raised her sights and identified the K2 gap. Now she had to decide on a strategy to achieve her new goals, which were to differentiate further as a tennis coach and launch a new venture in soccer coaching.

Cheryl decided that her strategy needed to be a blend of Stand Out! and Sharpen Up! She was going to build on her strengths, as well as address some of her potential weaknesses, specifically in management. She drew up three strategic alternatives. Alternative A was to upgrade her coaching technology skills, in particular learning how to edit video clips on a PC, by taking evening classes at Colorado Technical University (CTU). The investment cost would be a few hundred dollars, leading to a largely intangible benefit of nudging up Cheryl's K2 rating. But it would prepare her well for the Multi-Media scenario, should it happen.

Alternatives B and C related more to her soccer venture, Kickabout. Cheryl had no background in marketing or human resource management, and little in organization or finance, so she (and Chuck) believed it crucial for her to have some management training. One option was to undertake evening classes at CTU in specific management courses, such as marketing or accounting. These classes would not be expensive and should enable her to fit in alternative A at the same time.

Alternative C would be to go for goal and do a part-time MBA at CSSU. This would be a more costly investment and take much longer—probably three years. But it would give her huge confidence in setting up this and any other future venture.

She evaluated the three alternatives. Alternative A seemed a no-brainer, but it would be difficult to fit in if she took the alternative C route. The latter was the most exciting, and challenging, but would she be biting off more than she could chew? Would the MBA be too time-demanding while setting up her new venture? Would she have to postpone Kickabout? Friends of hers who had done part-time MBAs had found their lives overwhelmed by mountains of work. And would it over-qualify her for this modest business venture?

She decided it was premature to take on alternative C. Alternative B was lower cost, quicker, lower risk and could well yield more practical benefits of managing a small business than an MBA. It would also enable her to pursue alternative A simultaneously. B and A it was to be. C could wait for when Kickabout was ready for national roll-out and listing on the stock market!

Debi's Strategy

In the last chapter, we found that Debi had decided to go for goal. She had resolved to bridge the K2 gap by getting some training in marketing, improving her organizational skills, and learning how to speak in public. She recognized that her strategy was going to be more akin to Sharpen Up! than Stand Out!, but it was in marketing rather than reception work where she felt her passion lay.

Her strategic alternatives were fairly straightforward for the first two goals. She could choose from a range of evening courses in marketing at schools downtown or in Queens, where she lived, most of which were competitively priced. She would ask her office buddy, Su Ki, who was the most organized person Debi had ever met, if she would be her mentor in developing organizational skills.

But she was at a loss where to go to learn about public speaking. She didn't want to ask her colleagues. This was something she wanted to pursue in private. They could find out when, or if, she became an accomplished speaker. So she did some Googling and quickly found a one-week residential course in presentational skills and public speaking for $3,999. The Vermont country club setting sounded lovely, but what an investment! She also found a one-day, nonresidential course off Central Park for $650. Finally, she found a seemingly more cost-effective, ten-week, one-evening-per-week course at a Manhattan further education college for $289.

She figured that a one-day course was probably going to be a waste of time. She might learn what she was supposed to do, but there would be little chance for her to practice. The country club course was way beyond her budget, so she decided to try the local college for a few weeks (alternative A).

But ust before she sent off the check, she came across an ad in the classified section of an old issue of the *Queens Chronicle*. "Horrified at speaking in public?" it ran. "Join Toastmasters!" Odd name, Debi thought, but she called the toll-free anyway. Brilliant timing, she was told; a new club had recently been formed less than a mile away on Queens Boulevard and they were meeting the very next evening. She could come along as a guest, for free. What did she have to lose?!

From the moment Debi walked into the room, she felt the club reach out and embrace her. Each speaker was applauded and cheered, made to feel good. Each was evaluated in an amazingly positive and encouraging way. Members were learning to speak in a fun and astonishingly supportive environment. To her surprise—and initial terror—Debi was asked if she would give a one minute impromptu speech. Why not?! She thought she banged on a bit, in a rather random way, but she received such terrific applause when she sat down she felt like royalty!

Debi learned that the club met once a fortnight and would set her back all of $16 for the joining fee, followed by a mere $3 a month in membership dues! She didn't have to bother with the further education college and certainly not with the country club. Alternatives A or B? For the trash can! She'd found the solution. It had been on her doorstep all the time. And it was all but free!

A Word on Toastmasters International

What was this extraordinary organization Debi discovered? Does it exist in reality? Indeed it does and it's called Toastmasters International. There are 11,000 clubs worldwide, with 220,000 members. I've been a member since 1990, a founder member of London's second oldest club, London Corinthians Toastmasters. Over the years, I've seen scores of people transformed. I've seen petrified speakers learn to control their nerves and ultimately, incredibly, enjoy performing. I've seen dull speakers come alive. Good speakers become captivating.

Presentational and public speaking skills are initially like cycling or typing skills. They're not inherited, they can be learned. They're difficult at first to grasp, easier over time. Once learned, they become more like the golf swing— best kept tuned up through regular practice. Lack of practice can allow faults to creep in— whether swiping from the top in golf, or allowing hands to shield the face in speaking. Toastmasters is the ideal forum for such practice. There are hundreds—thousands—of real-life Debis whose work and social life has been uplifted by Toastmasters clubs across the world.

A chance ad meant that Debi didn't need to evaluate her strategic alternatives. She didn't even need an action plan. It was all too obvious. She just needed to turn up every other Thursday evening and her communications skills would improve, steadily and surely. Irreversibly. She pursued a strategy where the investment costs were not far off zero, the risks negligible, the payback immediate, and the returns astronomical.

For those readers who aren't members of Toastmasters, let me leave you with this thought: You're reading a book on career development, perhaps career change. You're clearly interested in self-development. There's no more effective program for self-development worldwide than Toastmasters International. Pop into www.toastmasters.org and click on "Find A Location Near You." Pick a convenient club and go along as a guest. You have nothing to lose. You'll come across a bunch of like-minded souls. At worst, you'll have a good evening's entertainment. For free.

At best, it'll transform your life.

In Short

What's your generic strategy? Here's a reminder:

- *Stand Out!*—Differentiate for success.

- *easyU!*—Become low cost for success.

- *Sharpen Act!*—Improve your competitiveness for partial success.

Which strategic alternative will best bridge the K2 gap?

Have you drawn up a realistic action plan?

13 Backing UCo?

*Nobody talks of entrepreneurship as survival,
but that's exactly what it is and what nurtures
creative thinking.*—Anita Roddick

One radical strategic alternative you may have considered in the last chapter is that of going it alone, of quitting your job to carry on providing more or less the same services, but under your own banner.

You'll form your own company, UCo. You'll set out to sell your services independently, perhaps initially to your former colleagues, now your customers, and subsequently to new customers. Or you may be entering into competition, whether direct or indirect, with your former company.

What are the pros and cons, the pitfalls, the risks, the opportunities, of UCo?

Going It Alone: Pros and Cons

First things first: I'm self-employed, and it ain't easy. If any reader thinks otherwise, you may be in for a rude awakening. Self-employment can be rewarding. It can help you achieve the work/life balance you seek. But don't make the mistake of thinking it's easy.

Let me give you more bad news, then I'll balance that with the good. Here are six reasons why setting up UCo may be tough.

It's not easy to win business. Most newly self-employed people have little experience of winning business. At their former company, they were typically handed work to do on a plate. Business was promoted by the marketing team and clinched by the sales team, with the company possessing a brand that conferred a degree of credibility in the sales process. Your role may have been to help deliver the business after it had been won. You will be new to selling.

You have to do everything yourself. When you're self-employed, who do you ask to type a letter? Issue an invoice? Then post it? Make the coffee? Keep the books? Wine and dine a key client? Chat up the local journalist? Design the business cards? Write the brochure? Provide content for the website? Choose the laptop? And the ISP? Delete the spam? Fix the abominable pop-ups? And, having done all that, provide the service better than the competition? The answer is scary: U! U! U! You're not just the CEO. You're also the GIC—gofer-in-chief.

There ain't no security. If you're an employee and you're feeling dreadful, with the flu or perhaps something nastier, what do you do? You call the boss and suggest, croakily, that you stay home for the day. You'll still receive your salary. Likewise if your son is unwell, your wife is unavailable, and you need to take him to the doctor, your bank account will still be credited at the end of the month. Just as it is when you're on holiday. An employee also has some element of job security. Not as much these days as in earlier decades, perhaps, but some.

There's none of that when you're self-employed. When you're sick, or when you have to care for sick relatives, you don't get paid. When you're on holiday, its cost is not offset by a salary check on your return. And there's no security, none at all, when the market gets tough. For the self-employed, you eat what you catch. No catch, no food. You are as we all once were: a hunter-gatherer.

Work time blurs into home time. For the self-employed, there becomes a finer distinction between when work stops and play starts. Work can infiltrate leisure time. This is especially true if you work from home. It can be difficult to turn off the laptop or put down your tools and play with the kids when there's work remaining undone.

It can be lonely. As CEO of UCo, you may be pretty isolated for much of the time. That comes with the territory. Worse, when things go badly, it can be lonely. Bad news like a lost pitch can be hard to take. It gets more personal. It's not your company the client is rejecting in favor of another provider. It's you. It's your skills, your track record, your storyline, your pricing, your personality, your face, your armpits (?!), your everything. In a word, you. It can be tough.

Don't do it for the money. It's a common fallacy that self-employed people make more than employees. It's not generally the case. Just because the daily rates may seem high, remember they are multiplied not by 5*52 days/year, but by the days you do paid work per year—a very different concept. Take off days for marketing, pitching, admin, holidays, or sickness, and take off days for downtime/ no work—and your annual earnings may not be spectacular.

Phew! So much for the disadvantages; now let's try to redress the balance. Here are some of the main advantages of being self-employed, of being the head honcho of UCo!

You're your own boss. This is the most obvious boon. No reporting, no asking for permission, no annual reviews, no internal politics. No need to account to anyone but U! To those of us with little patience for bosses of limited capability other than playing the corporate game of slippery snakes and greasy ladders, this is a big plus.

You'll grow your business. Each time you win a new customer, that's your precious customer. Each time you receive payment, that's your bank account you'll be dropping the check into. Each time you prepare your annual accounts, hopefully you'll be tracking the growth of your company, your enterprise, your initiative, your energy. Your baby. It feels good.

You can select your own free time. This is the flipside to the disadvantage above of work slipping into leisure time. Leisure can also slip happily into work time when you're self-employed. You're bashing away at the laptop, the lad comes home from school and he wants to kick a ball with you in the park. Why not?!

You'll see more of the family. Few self-employed people have long commutes. Many work from home or from nearby offices, maybe just down the road. Many visit other people's homes within a reasonable radius of theirs. Time saved in commuting should mean more time with the family. When you see both parents of a child at an after lunch performance of the school's jazz band, what's the betting that the working parent (or parents) is self-employed?

So there you have it. Some fantastic advantages to being self-employed, balanced by some rather grim disadvantages. It's a lifestyle choice. Over to you!

If you do decide to go for it, here are some tips on how to make UCo a success.

It's All About Selling and Marketing

If no one knows you're there, you won't get any business. No matter how good you are at what you do.

If you're from a sales background, you'll have a head start on forming UCo. Even if there are many others out there much better at doing the work, you could well do better than they. You'll know how to make customers aware of your offering, and why it's the best option for them.

If, however, you're like most of us who have gone it alone, and you've had very little experience in selling and marketing, then please take one thing away from this section: *Seek help!*

Consider postponing any plans you may have had to further develop your offering. Learn instead how to sell. It'll open your eyes. Learn the most effective ways to market your type of service.

Read a few books. Enroll in a course. Or engage some help. Meanwhile, here are some tips I've learned along the way. They may not be comprehensive, like in larger tomes on sales and marketing, but do these and you'll be well on the way.

Perfect your elevator speech! You need to be absolutely clear about what it is you offer and why it delivers distinctive benefits to your clients. All in one simple sentence. It should be able to be delivered, if necessary, when meeting a stranger in an elevator between the first and third floors!

Reinforce your message! Don't just send a client a letter, a leaflet, or a business card. Certainly don't just shoot her an email. Call her. Knock on her door. Get yourself in a newspaper or journal talking about your business and its benefits. Bump into her at networking events. Get another client to speak highly of you to her. Let her be bombarded with your message by hearing it from many different sources.

Try 10-Touch Marketing! Let your client be reminded of your existence and your message 10 times during each year—that's more or less once a month, excluding the summer holidays. The touches can range from sending a Christmas card to a two-hour PowerPoint presentation, from a catch-up call to a liquid lunch on a Friday, from an email with an interesting attachment to a piece of business. But try to make it a 10-touch year for each key client.

Pick up that phone! Why are so many self-employed people shy when it comes to picking up the phone? Too bad. We have no choice. If you hate calling as much as I do, here are six tips that have helped me: prepare your pitch in advance; psych yourself up before the call; stand up to make the call; have something to say that she will find interesting (or preferably amusing); reinforce anything that you and she may have in common; and, at the end of the call, angle for some follow-up action. Finally, invest in a good answering machine (or voice-mail) to handle the return call that comes in just when your hands are fiddling with a diaper.

Don't be shy about asking for referrals and testimonials! There's no better way of getting an introduction to a prospective client than being referred to him by an existing, satisfied client. That's a referral, and it's the lifeblood of the self-employed. Best of all is when your client will actually call up the prospect, or mention you next time he sees him. Next best is when your client gives you a testimonial extolling your capabilities. This you can put into a letter to the prospect and follow it up with a phone call a few days later. Still good is when your client just says "Sure, you can use my name" and you call up the prospect saying, "So-and-so suggested I give you a call." Don't be shy asking for referrals. You should ask every client for them.

Don't be greedy! When you realize you're in pole position to win a piece of work, don't blow it by being greedy. Remember it's better to be utilized and earning something than unutilized and earning nothing. Give good service at a good price. That'll be doubly good value to the customer. And he'll use you again.

If you have to, use an agent! If you've read books on sales and marketing, been to a seminar or two, tried out some of the tips above, and you still aren't selling as much as someone with your capabilities should be delivering, try an agent. Find someone who's a professional salesperson, preferably with some good contacts. Someone with boundless energy and a passion for selling. Such people do exist! Payment of 10 percent, even 15 percent commission on sales should more than repay itself, compared with the alternative of you remaining underutilized.

The final word on selling and marketing yourself should rest, perhaps slightly out of context, with the inimitable Mae West: "It's better to be looked over than overlooked."

More Tips

Sales and marketing will be the most important function in UCo. But it's not the only one. Here are some more tips.

Don't forget the delivery. It goes without saying that you must be especially good at your job if you're going to be self employed. Unlike for an employee, there's no one to hide behind. You're on your own, totally exposed. Ideally you'll be ready for top-notch service delivery from the day you launch. Then all you need to do is bring in the business and deliver quality work.

Then there's the admin. Unfortunately there's more to running your own business than selling and delivering. There's the red tape. Admin work must be kept under control, yet it mustn't eat into too much of your sales and delivery time. It's a delicate balance, one that will come with experience, and the odd mistake.

Stash the cash! There's one admin task, however, which takes precedence over all others. Revenues are great, but they don't pay the bills. Cash does that, and it needs collecting. By you. Cash management is often quoted in surveys as one of the main reasons why small businesses fail. No matter how marvelous the market, how brilliant your business concept, if you run out of cash, your business is bust.

Where's your support? We saw earlier that lack of support of colleagues is a major disadvantage of being self-employed. The self-employed need a support system in place to compensate. What will yours be in UCo? Suppose you faced hard times, how would you cope? You need to tee up your lines of support, be they family, friends, associates, or a bank manager prepared to extend adequate credit.

Still thinking of UCo? Be aware that it's no bed of roses. But then nowhere is. UCo, on balance, is the place for me. How about U?

In Short

Could your strategy be UCo?

Don't think it's going to be a picnic.

Learn how to sell. And stash the cash!

14 More Backable?

*I believe the true road to pre-eminent success
in any line is to make yourself master in that line.
I have no faith in the policy of scattering one's
resources, and in my experience I have rarely
if ever met a man who achieved preeminence
in money making...who was interested in
many concerns.*—Andrew Carnegie

Are U now more backable? Take another look at the risks and opportunities of backing U that were assessed in Chapter 8. How have they changed as a result of your new strategy of Chapter 12 (which may have led to forming UCo, as in Chapter 13)?

Are some of the risks now less likely? Or with lower impact? Have new risks been introduced by pursuing your new strategy? If so, are they containable?

What about the opportunities? Are they now more likely? Or with higher impact? Has your new strategy identified new opportunities? How promising?

Do the big opportunities surpass the big risks more so than in Chapter 8?

They should. That's what your strategy was designed for.

If, however, you weren't absolutely convinced in Part I that you were backable in your current job or business, and if in Part II those doubts weren't fully lain to rest, then you should move on to Part III. Perhaps you should consider switching to a new career, one where the passion lies.

Is Cheryl More Backable?

In Chapter 8, Chuck identified one "big" risk in backing Cheryl, namely that she had no experience in managing and marketing an organization. In Chapter 12, Cheryl decided to enroll in evening classes in marketing and accounting at Colorado Technical University prior to the launch of Kickabout. That big risk was now both less likely, and less big.

She also decided to strengthen her standing as a tennis coach by taking video editing classes. This was a new opportunity.

Cheryl's strategy had improved the balance of risk and opportunity before her. She was now even more backable. Chuck was onto a winner.

Is Debi More Backable?

Chuck identified in Chapter 8 one big risk in backing Debi—that she would so neglect her receptionist role in pursuing a marketing role that she could end up losing both. But Debi was prepared to take this risk head on. In Chapter 10 she determined to raise her sights and go for goal. She drew up in Chapter 12 an ambitious strategy: She would undertake evening classes in marketing, take on a mentor to improve her organizational

Musical Shuttles

A high-profile entrepreneur is planning to launch a space tourism business in 2010. That's about as risky a venture as can be imagined. But he has defied conventional wisdom often before. While immersed in the music business in the mid-1980s, he launched, to general astonishment, a transatlantic airline. It still thrives. Other diverse ventures have prospered likewise. His success can be partly attributable to a consistent, focused strategy: delivering quality value for money to the customer, dashed with a frisson of excitement. Who would bet against him succeeding with *Virgin Galactic?*

skills, and join Toastmasters to learn how to speak in public.

The big risk remained. But it was offset by a new opportunity—a focused strategy on how Debi could succeed in a marketing role. She was going for goal. Chuck was impressed. She was now more backable.

In Short

Has your new strategy made you less risky?

Are U now more backable?

Part III
Backing the *Hwyl!*

Introduction

Twenty years from now you will be more disappointed by the things that you didn't do than by the ones you did. So throw off the bowlines. Sail away from the safe harbor. Catch the trade winds in your sails. Explore. Dream. Discover.—Mark Twain

If you concluded in Part I that you would not, or probably would not, back U in your current job or business, then Part III helps you to find a field where you would back U. It shows you how to back the *hwyl*, the Celtic concept of passion, fervor, and spirit, which can lift you to extremes of success. (By the way, don't be disheartened by the apparent absence of vowels in *hwyl!* The word actually contains two vowels! There are seven vowels in the Welsh language, the familiar five as in English plus "w" and "y." *Hwyl* is pronounced as in who-yl.)

Part III starts with the discovery of passion, or *hwyl*. Chapter 15, Wherein Lies the

Hwyl?, helps you draw up a long list of jobs or businesses where your passion lies. This list is screened in Chapter 16, Screening for Reality, down to a short list of three or four jobs that not only have *hwyl* but also where you could succeed.

In Chapter 17, Where Best to Back?, you'll be guided on how to assess which of these shortlisted fields is the most promising—using the tools set out in Part I. Then in Chapter 18, you'll develop a strategy to improve your chances of success in your target job—using the tools of Part II. Finally, in Chapter 19, Now Back the *Hwyl!,* we'll look at some key steps you need to take to land your job with *hwyl.*

Part III will show you how to find the right job or business with *hwyl* and improve your prospects of getting in and succeeding there. Hopefully it will inspire you to get out there and back your *hwyl!*

> *All the things I love is what my business is all about.*—Martha Stewart

15 Wherein Lies the *Hwyl?*

Life is to be lived. If you have to support yourself, you had bloody well better find some way that is going to be interesting.—Katherine Hepburn

This chapter helps you to find the field of work where your passion lies. Whose job, or business, do you most covet? If you were in that business, you would be so fired up that work wouldn't seem like work at all. The job would fill you with *hwyl.*

It doesn't matter at this stage whether you think you could actually do this job, run this business. The important thing is to imagine what you would love to be doing in your day job. You'll be given some tips on how you can come up with dozens of jobs with *hwyl.* Then you'll be shown how to pull out a dozen or so of those jobs with the most *hwyl,* ready to be screened in the next chapter.

A *Hwyl*-Driven Approach to Career Change

Many excellent books guide you through a bottom-up, skills-driven approach to career change (see the Appendix to this book). *Backing U! LITE* suggests a different approach, one that is top-down, demand-pulled, *hwyl*-driven. Instead of working bottom-up from what your values, interests, and skills are, it starts top-down with where you'd like to end up.

What job would you love to have? In which job would you be happy?

Which job can you think of where work would no longer be "work"? You would be so fired up it wouldn't seem like work at all. You would rush to work in the morning and you wouldn't want to leave in the evening.

Who would you most like to be? Whose job, or business, do you most covet? If you were in his or her job, would you have your dream job?

In which job would you be consumed with *hwyl*? You would feel such passion, such fervor, such spirit, you would be uplifted to extremes of success.

That's the top-down approach. It's demand driven, in that it seeks to pinpoint those magnetic jobs that attract you to them, that draw you toward them. It's not the supply pushed approach, where you steer yourself toward a job that suits your values, interests, and skills

And it's driven by *hwyl*. The job will entice you with its promise of *hwyl*.

How to Know Where the *Hwyl* Lies?

You'll know when you've found a job with *hwyl*. Just thinking about it is exciting. It'll make your thoughts race. It'll wake you at five o'clock in the morning, and you won't want to go back to sleep.

It'll fill you with drive. To do something about it. To pick up the phone, knock on a door.

> ### Ho$ting
>
> A part-time model during her university days at Barnard, where she studied history and architectural history, this daughter of Polish Americans became a successful stockbroker. She quit in her early thirties to become a full-time mother, while undertaking a major restoration of her early 19th century farmhouse. There she loved to entertain family and friends, so much so that she figured she should make a career of it. From her basement she launched a catering business, and after a couple of years produced a cookbook. *Entertaining* became a best seller and paved the way to a multimedia lifestyle phenomenon. She had found the *hwyl.*

Above all, you'll know you've found the *hwyl* when you speak about the job. When people talk about something they're passionate about, the voice changes. The pace quickens. The pitch rises. The volume gets turned up a notch or two.

Try talking about the job to a friend. Talk about its daily routines, the kind of people who work there, their ambitions, their achievements. Its pros and cons. Talk about it in relation to other jobs where the *hwyl* may also lie. Talk about how it differs from ordinary jobs, why it inspires you more than your current job. Ask your friend to observe how you talk about these jobs. When you speak of this dream job, does your voice become faster, more animated, more impassioned?

The *hwyl* will be reflected in the voice. If you speak about a job where the *hwyl* lies, your voice will confirm it.

But how to find such a job?

Some Tips on Finding Where the *Hwyl* Lies

The problem with the top-down approach, I can hear some argue, is in getting started. Suppose you have never heard of or come across the ideal job for you! How can you envision it and then work out whether you're suited for it?

They're right! For some people, this may well be so. In which case, please revert to the bottom-up approach. Set out your values, interests, and transferable skills and work up from there.

In the majority of cases, however, the top-down approach should work too because you already know of, or you can get to know of, the kind of work you would like to do. That's not to decry the bottom-up approach, of course. It's proven. It works.

How to find the ideal job for you? How to discover where the *hwyl* lies? If you don't already know, and many of you do, here are some tips.

Whose jobs do you admire of those you know? Think of your family. Your friends. Your old school friends. Your colleagues. Your former colleagues. Your kids' friends' parents. Are any of them in a job or running a business that would inspire you? Have they been in the past? Are they thinking of switching to one? Take one further degree of separation: What about the family, friends, and colleagues of your family, friends, and colleagues? Do they have jobs that would inspire you?

Take a piece of paper and make three

columns. In the left-hand column, write down all the names you've just thought of. In the middle column, write down the kind of work these people do, or did. Then in the right-hand column, indicate to what extent the work would inspire you. Try ticks. Or a cross for a job that does nothing for you. One tick for an okay job. Two ticks for a good job. Three ticks for a great job.

Then give four, five, or however many ticks you can fit across the column for the jobs that would truly inspire you—the jobs where the *hwyl* lies.

What jobs do your fellow interest-sharers do? Do you belong to any clubs, societies, voluntary groups, political groups? Your fellow members in these clubs share at least one thing in common with you, their interest in the purpose of that organization. All of you in that group like, for example, golf, or books, or ballroom dancing. Might there be something else you have in common with these people, other than the one common interest through which you know each other? Might you have *work* interests in common? Are any of them in a job that would inspire you? What about *their* family, friends, and colleagues?

Take out your sheet of paper and add to it some jobs of your fellow interest-sharers and their contacts.

Do you know a dozen people who found the hwyl? Who do you know who has changed careers successfully in their lives? Not many? I bet that's not so. I'm sure you could list a dozen or so with ease. Have any of these career switches been of interest to you? Inspired you? Ask your friends, family, fellow club/society members to rattle off a dozen examples likewise. You could soon have well over a hundred exemplars! Any inspiration there?

Who do you know of whose work inspires you? So far you've looked to people you know for inspiration. Now take a look at people you don't know but you know *of.* Think of people you've read about in books who have inspired you. Think of people you've looked at or read about in newspapers, in the supplements, in magazines. Think of people you've seen on TV. In documentaries, in reality shows, in sports, on the news. People who've inspired you in some way. Think too of fictitious people. People in novels, in movies, in the theater, in dramas, or soaps on TV. People whose imaginary lives have come alive for you through fiction or drama. Try broadening your reading to gain further inspiration.

Consult a list. We're starting to scrape the barrel a bit here. If you haven't found inspiration from any of the above sources, it's unlikely that a dry, factual, unemotional list of (thousands of) occupations is going to inspire. But you never know. Try the U.S. Bureau of Labor Statistics website (www bls.gov).

Take a career test. This route belongs more to the bottom-up approach, but you might try one or two for interest—there are plenty on the web.

Your Long List of a Dozen Jobs With *Hwyl*

The time has come to review your list. Take out your sheet of paper and see what you've come up with. You may have before you a list of two, three, or more dozen jobs that could inspire you to varying degrees. Now the list needs to be made more manageable.

Rearrange the full list (easier if you've typed it out on your word processor) by grouping the jobs by the number of ticks received. At the very top, group together all those jobs that gained five or more ticks. Then those with four, three, and so on. Last, and least, should be those with crosses.

Now you weed out those with the fewest ticks. Obviously, you'll start with all the crosses. Then you'll move up to the single ticks. Carry on this process until you have only a dozen or so jobs left. Hopefully these final dozen will each have received at least three ticks.

No more than a dozen jobs are needed at this stage. You can always return to the list if you have to. A dozen is a reasonably sized list to be taking into the next chapter on screening. This is your *long list* of jobs with *hwyl*.

To reiterate: At this stage, it doesn't matter whether you could do these jobs well, or if you even qualify to do them. The important thing is to derive a manageable long list of jobs that inspire you, ranked purely by the extent to which they will fill you with *hwyl*.

Roger's Long List

Roger, whom we met briefly in the introduction to this book, is a self-employed IT consultant in his late forties and works from home in Vancouver. He was one of the many victims of the dot-com bubble burst in 2001 and has since combined periods of subcontracting with a local Mr. PC Fixit business. It hasn't been easy, with competition tough in all his areas of IT expertise. He approached Chuck Cash for backing and was unsuccessful. These were Chuck's findings, Chapter 9-style.

Roger's position in IT services in Vancouver seems vulnerable and he should seriously research teaching or other lower risk opportunities:

- *Market demand prospects*—Demand for IT services in Vancouver has recovered from the downturn of 2000–2003 and is growing steadily, while demand growth for home PC fixit services has slowed as PC household penetration approaches saturation.
- *Competition*—Competition was intense in 2000–2003, with a chronic over-supply of IT professionals, but has eased since—though every year hundreds more youngsters join the market and put pressure on their more mature peers.
- *Roger's K2 rating*—Roger is a highly experienced IT consultant, but his enthusiasm has waned, along with preparedness to work long hours, and

he may no longer be staying ahead of the game technically.

- *Roger's plan*—Roger's plans to maintain his current level of profits may be challenging, and he should consider trading off a cut in earnings for a job with greater security.
- *Risks and opportunities*—Competition and attitude risks seem to outweigh opportunities for Roger in his current business—he should research lower risk jobs like teaching, in which he has expressed some interest.

With that storyline, Chuck wasn't going to back Roger. He was too risky. Roger had had a rough five or six years, with prolonged periods of low utilization and earnings, and they have taken their toll. He now acts as if he's semi-retired, partially exited from the labor market. His competitors are more active, more assertive, younger.

The teaching retraining opportunity could be a lifeline for Roger. The state government needs scores of IT teachers to go into elementary schools, but the work is not perceived as attractive to many young, bright, dollar-hungry IT professionals—the very types who have been competing ferociously with Roger in his current work. But is this really what Roger wants to do?

Chuck suggests that Roger should go back to square one. What would he love to do? What would inspire him? What would fill him with *hwyl?* How would teaching compare?

Roger takes a look at this chapter for assessing where the *hwyl* lies. No problem, there. He has been thinking about his career options so much in recent years that he comes up with a full list of 40 jobs right off the bat.

What Roger finds most interesting is the *hwyl* rating. There's no doubt which job merits the full five ticks. Roger was a keen actor at his university dramatic club and did some amateur dramatics in his early twenties, before pressures of work and family took over. He would still love to be an actor, preferably on stage in front of a live, vibrant, youthful audience, rather than perform to a sterile camera lens on screen or TV.

But he's in his late forties and surely it's too late now to embark on a professional acting career? He calls Chuck. "You may well be right," says Chuck, "and the acting job may be screened out in the next chapter. But the important thing at this stage is to establish a *hwyl* benchmark, against which all other jobs can be assessed. If acting gets five ticks, which jobs get four?" Roger thanks Chuck and presses on.

He finds that just 15 of the 40 jobs on his full list merit three ticks or more. He's curious and amused to find that lying behind acting's five ticks is a motley collection of six jobs with four ticks, ranging from a country-western singer-songwriter, a bar owner/manager, a coach driver, and a softball coach to a funeral parlor manager (his brother-in-law's fellow chorister finds it fulfilling).

The sixth job with four ticks, Roger is

happy to find, is teaching. The old maxim that teachers are frustrated actors, performing daily before a small audience, seems apposite. He also likes the idea of introducing kids to the wonders of IT. But is it a bit late in life to be taking on the pressures and stress experienced by many teachers?

Selina's Long List

We also met Selina at the start of this book. She's in her late twenties and manages the children's department at Thomas Ellis & Co, an old-fashioned department store in Stratford-upon-Avon. After discussions with Chuck, these were his Chapter 9–style conclusions.

Selina seems a capable retail manager, but faces employment risk, a possible attitude risk, and constraints on job mobility—though her new venture idea sounds promising.

- *Market demand prospects*—Demand for fashion retail sales staff in Stratford seems be growing steadily, but demand for shopping at the anachronistic Thomas Ellis & Co may be on the wane.
- *Competition*—Competition for sales staff seems moderate, with supply growth limited by the steady exodus of youth to nearby cities and London, but the highly dated Ellis's seems vulnerable to competition from fashion chains, boutiques, mail order, and Internet shopping.
- *Selina's K2 rating*—Selina is an

excellent salesperson, a competent manager of the children's department and worthy of promotion, but she is frustrated at Ellis's.

- *Selina's plan*—Selina has set financial targets well above her current earnings, which could be met in London were the family to relocate.
- *Risks and opportunities*—The major risks facing Selina are the possible insolvency of Ellis's, her attitude there and family constraints on job mobility, but the children's boutique venture seems an opportunity worth researching.

Chuck wouldn't back her in her current job, because he wasn't sure what he would be backing. Was he backing a good manager in an organization that could be heading for trouble? In which case, the answer was no. Was he backing a good manager who had been head-hunted to work in a higher paid job in London, but whose husband was reluctant to relocate? If so, ditto. Or was he backing a prospective children's boutique entrepreneur? If so, where's the plan? And was she sure this was what she wanted to do? Was this where the passion lay? Where else? "Prove your case!" urged Chuck.

Selina studies this chapter. She looks at the jobs done by her family, her neighbors, her high school buddies, her aerobics classmates, her kids' friends' parents, as well as friends and family of all of them. Then she thinks of those she has read about or seen on TV who have inspired her. In a couple of days she has drawn up a full list of 54 jobs and businesses.

Once rated and sorted, 18 jobs emerge with at least three *hwyl* ticks, and just 10 with four or more ticks. These are to be her long list. They are an eclectic bunch, from the London Megastore manager job offer to a children's TV presenter, a manager at a travel industry PR firm, and managing a Stratford-based human rights charity.

The only two jobs with five ticks, Selina is delighted to discover, are her children's boutique venture and setting up with a friend a daycare/preschool center for three-month to five-year old kids. Clearly she's passionate about becoming an entrepreneur in a child-centric environment. She looks forward to seeing how these jobs fare in Chapter 16's screening.

In Short

Draw up a full list of jobs with varying degrees of *hwyl*.

Rearrange by order of *hwyl*.

Take the top dozen or so as your long list.

16 Screening for Reality

Follow your own particular dreams. We are handed a life by peers, parents and society, you can do that or follow your own dreams. Life is short, be a dreamer but be a practical person.—Hugh Hefner

In the last chapter, you derived a long list of a dozen or so jobs or businesses you would love to do. These were careers with *hwyl*. Some of these jobs you may stand little chance of getting into, let alone succeeding in them. A shame, but that's life. Others you may do well in. The purpose of this chapter is to derive a short list of two or three jobs. These will not only be jobs with *hwyl* but also jobs in which you could succeed.

You'll do very little extra research in this chapter. That's for the next one. Here you'll take a first cut at assessing how attractive the markets are for each of these jobs and how well placed you would be to get in and succeed in them. You'll effectively be doing a quick and dirty assessment of how backable you'd be in each job.

Screening for Backability

The screening process has to be as objective as you can make it. The aim is not to provide you with a clearer ranking of which job you'd most like to do. It's to find out in which job you could be *backable*. Out of all those jobs with *hwyl*, where would a backer consider you worth a punt?

This aim has implications for the criteria we'll use in ranking the jobs. Typically, when people are thinking of a career change, they'll list criteria such as pay, working conditions, values, culture, location, type of colleague, status, and so forth. They'll use these criteria to rank possible careers by relative attractiveness.

This is all highly valid. But it's not for here. It's for the next chapter, *after* we've screened the long list for backability.

There is little point in spending loads of time doing further research on a career where it's highly unlikely that you'll be backable. To a real-life Chuck Cash.

How Attractive (Roughly) Are the Markets for These Jobs?

The first thing we need to consider, from the perspective of a prospective backer, as in Part I, is how attractive are the markets for these jobs.

Gut feel is what's needed at this stage. You need to rank your long list by what you feel. You already have a vague notion of market demand and competition for these jobs, because you know something about them. These are jobs to which you aspire, where you believe the *hwyl* lies. Let your gut provide a preliminary view.

You need to rank each of the long-listed jobs or businesses by four criteria:

- *Number of people engaged in this job or business*—Are there many people working in this field, compared to the numbers engaged in other fields?
- *Growth in jobs or businesses*—Is this a field where there will be growing demand for people over the next few years? Or is demand more likely to stay flat, or decline?
- *Competition for jobs or among businesses*—How ferocious is the competition to get these jobs? To what extent does the supply of people wanting to do these jobs exceed vacancies available? If this is a business, how intense is the competition between businesses? Is it intensifying?
- *Job market risk*—How risky is this job or business, compared to others?

Take care to get the rankings of job market attractiveness the right way round (!):
- The more jobs available, the more attractive the market.
- The faster the growth, the more attractive the market.
- The more competitive, the less attractive the market.
- The more risky, the less attractive the market.

How attractive are your long-listed jobs overall? One or two on your long list may already be screened out. If market conditions are unfavorable, you're unlikely to be backable. You'll be pushing uphill. But others on the list should come through okay.

What Would Be Your K2 Rating (Roughly) in These Jobs?

The second stage of the screening process is to assess how well placed you would be to get in and then succeed at this job or business.

Gut feel is again all that's needed at this stage. For each job or business, think of your K2 rating being determined by two criteria only:

- Your relevant capabilities—How you would rate against the capabilities required for the job or business?
- Your experience—How you would rate against the experience needed to do the job or run the business?

The first criterion relates to how well you think you would do the job, or run the business, if you got into it. How relevant are your skills, your innate talents, to the skills needed to perform the job successfully? How suitable are your qualifications?

The second criterion is important in those jobs or businesses where experience is a serious barrier to entry. There may be a whole range of jobs you know you could do well, but your lack of relevant experience would make you hard to back. Not necessarily because you couldn't do the job. More because prospective employers, or indeed your customers, would be looking for someone more experienced than you to be offering and delivering such a service.

Some words of warning on the experience rating:

- When screening a long list, you may think you have no experience at all of doing a particular job. Don't be dismayed. Think about what elements of your experience to date may at least be indirectly or tangentially relevant to that job.
- Remember that we're looking primarily for relative comparisons, not absolute levels. We're looking for jobs where some aspects of your past experience may be more relevant than for others.
- If you're young, say under 30 (lucky you!), the experience criterion may be less relevant than for those of us who are not so young, especially for the over-fifties. Youngsters applying for jobs are typically assessed less rigorously on experience than on capability. And on *potential* capability.

Again, one or two jobs on your long list will now be screened out. If you really have few of the required capabilities and little experience for the job you covet, it's better to axe it now rather than later. But in others your rough K2 rating may emerge reasonably okay as it passes through the screen.

How Backable Would You Be in These Jobs?

Now we need to combine your rough assessment of market attractiveness with your similarly rough assessment of your K2 rating. Which job or business came through the screen as being (roughly) in the most attractive markets *and* with your highest (simplified) K2 rating?

If there's no clear winner, which job or business came through very well in market attraction and reasonably well in K2 rating? Or vice-versa—reasonably well in market attractiveness, very well in K2 rating?

These seem likely to be your most backable jobs. But which gained the most *hwyl* ticks in the last chapter?

Your two or three short-listed jobs are the ones where you are most backable, defined by market attractiveness and K2 rating, as well as offering you the most *hwyl*.

Another Iteration?

Suppose no jobs manage to pass through your screening? That is entirely possible. After all, when you drew up your long list of jobs with *hwyl* you took no account whatsoever of your capability to do them. Many of those jobs at the top of your long list are just wishful thinking, and that's fine. Once you take account of your ability to do the job or your relevant experience, many will be screened out. This is tough, but hardly surprising. We'd all love to be movie stars, but realistically we're not all going to make it from here!

Don't be deterred. Try another iteration. Go back to your long list and import the next dozen or so jobs. Pass them through the screening process. One or two may well emerge the other end. Still short of the two or three jobs needed for a short list? Try one more iteration and pull across another dozen jobs. Hopefully by now you'll have found two or three that are sufficiently promising to merit the short list.

You've screened your long list down to a short list of jobs that not only have *hwyl* but where you may also be backable. They need to be further researched in the next chapter.

Roger's Screening

Roger's long list of 15 jobs included one with five ticks, six with four, and the rest just three ticks. His five-ticked job was sadly the first to be screened out. Market prospects for actors were tough enough, but Roger's lack of experience (for his age), coupled with only average capability—truth be told he was no Laurence Olivier—meant it had to go. Chuck wouldn't back him as an actor.

Next to go were his country-western aspirations, screened out as being competitively intense. Screening for his likely (rough) K2 rating also took out managing a funeral parlor, where his lack of managerial experience would constrain his backability.

Best placed after the screening process were teaching, and more surprisingly, coach driving. Market conditions for the latter seemed good, with many vacancies advertised, and Roger's clean driving record and many years' experience of long distance family holidays in the RV should hold him in good stead. Applying the *hwyl* factor, his three ticks for coach driving (he found long distance driving relaxing, unlike urban driving) fell short of teaching's four ticks, so it would be the latter to proceed to the next chapter for further research, with coach driving as a fall-back.

Selina's Screening

Selina had come up with a long list of 10 jobs or businesses, each of which had registered at least four *hwyl* ticks. One of them was screened out immediately in terms of market attractiveness: TV presenting was known to be ferociously competitive. A shame, thought Selina, who'd have loved to present children's programs. Also screened out was the Megastore job in London, given her husband's reticence to relocate. More were screened out in terms of her likely K2 rating, including TV presenting again—she really had no relevant experience! Also screened out, regrettably, was her five *hwyl*-ticked preschool center idea, where her experience with her own children and selling children's clothes weren't relevant enough.

The two clear leaders from the screening were her children's boutique idea and a management role at David Morgan & Co, a more modernized competitor to Thomas Ellis & Co in Stratford. The boutique had more exciting market prospects, but Selina's managerial experience would make her more backable at Morgan's.

But once Selina applied the *hwyl* factor, there was no doubting that the boutique, with its five tick rating, should be the winner. The four tick Morgan's option, where Selina would remain an employee, could be a stand-by.

In Short

Screen your long list by (rough) market attractiveness and (rough) K2 rating

Draw up your short list of two or three jobs with *hwyl*

17 Where Best to Back?

*I always wanted to be somebody, but I should
have been more specific.*—Lily Tomlin

In the last chapter, you short-listed the
most promising two or three jobs or businesses with *hwyl*. You took a long list, applied screening criteria and emerged with a
short list of potentially backable jobs with
hwyl. In this chapter, you need to do some
serious research. It should lead you to the
most promising job or business with *hwyl*,
the ideal job that's waiting out there for you.
The target job.

There are three main areas where you
need to do further research before you can
draw firm conclusions:

- How satisfying would these short-
listed jobs be for you?
- How attractive really are the markets
for these jobs?
- How well placed really would you be
in these jobs?

Let's take them one at a time.

How Satisfying Are These Jobs for You?

Let's recap. The two or three jobs or businesses that have made it into your short list are those that inspire you, fill you with *hwyl*. Hopefully they will be among those to which you gave four or five ticks in Chapter 15.

But how much do you *really* know about them? How well paid are they? Do you have to excel to make good money? What are the working conditions like? Will your desk be near a window? Will you have to work long hours? Where will you work? Will you have to spend long periods away from your family? What sort of work will you actually do? Will that be fulfilling? What values will your colleagues have? Will they be compatible with yours? What status will this job have in the community? Is that important to you?

You won't yet have answers to many of these questions. But you need to know. And now's the time to find out.

First you need to establish what constitutes satisfaction in a job or business for you personally? What would make you satisfied in your job? Loads of money? Perhaps, but at what cost? Would you accept bucketfuls of bucks every day if it meant you were expected to work in unhealthy or unsafe conditions? What if you had to compromise—even abandon—your ethics? What if it meant being entirely self-centered, with no regard for others less fortunate? What if you had to bury your true self, contain your sense of humor? What if you had to be cavalier with the law?

For most people, there are many diverse

aspects of job satisfaction to take into account, not just hoarding the gold. Job satisfaction criteria can be grouped under six heads:

- *Pay*—Is this job (or business) likely to meet or exceed your desired level of wages or salary? And pension?
- *Working conditions*—Will this job meet your expectations of type of work, hours of work, independence, work/life balance, location, frequency of overnight travel, and other working conditions?
- *Fulfillment*—Will this type of work enable you to fulfill your manual, intellectual, and creative talents?
- *Values*—Will the culture of the organization, the nature of the work, the character of your colleagues be compatible with your values?
- *Status*—Would this job confer the status you require, whether to your own self-esteem or to the community?
- Hwyl—Will this job inspire you, fill you with passion, fervor, spirit? Joy? Fun?

So far, you've ranked prospective jobs or businesses using only the last criterion, *hwyl*. It's the best place to start, but it's now time to see whether your short-listed jobs measure up to your other job satisfaction criteria.

First you need to decide which job satisfaction criteria matter most to you. How does pay rank? What level of importance—high, low, or medium? Do the same for each criterion.

Then consider to what extent each short-listed job will satisfy each criterion. Will job A pay more than job B? Will it be more fulfilling? Do the same for each criterion.

Now assess those ratings against the level of importance you gave earlier to each criterion. Which job would give you greatest overall satisfaction?

It may be difficult to make sensible comparative assessments at this stage. To get a firmer rating will require further research. You'll get some guidance on how to do that later in this chapter in: *How to find out?*

It's Back to Part I for the Target Job, Plus a Backup

It's now time for some serious research. You need to repeat, more or less, Part I of this book. Not for your *current* job or business, but for your *target*.

At the same time you should do some limited, desk-based research on a backup job, the runner-up in the short-listing. This should give you work enough to be getting on with as you dig up data, talk to people, and build the storyline.

If further research suggests that the target job may not be suitable for you, then at least you have a backup. You can upgrade research on the backup job to full Part I analysis, while starting desk-based research on the third placed job. And so on, always keeping a backup if prospects for your target job fade away.

How Attractive Are the Markets Really for Your Target Job?

The first main area for further research is market attractiveness. You need to firm up on the rough assessment you made for Chapter 16's screening process. You know how to do it. You've already done it once in Chapters 2 and 3 for your current job or business. You just need to go through the process again, step by step, for the target job.

Research on market demand and competition will be trickier than last time round, since you may barely know this target market. It will be hard work but worth it. It has to be done if you are to convince Chuck you should switch to a backable career where the *hwyl* lies.

How Well Placed Would You Really Be for These Jobs?

Next you need to firm up on how well placed you would be in this target job or business. You need to confirm the rough assessment you undertook during Chapter 16's screening process.

Again, you know how to do it. You've already done it once in Chapters 4, 5, and 6 for your current job or business. You just need to do it again, for the target job.

Don't be dismayed if your K2 rating comes out low; it may be because of your lack of experience. Think about what your rating could be *in three years' time.* By then, the gulf in experience between you and those presently in the job will have narrowed.

And remember there's one Key Kapability where you'll be at least on a par with those already in the field. And hopefully you may out-shine many of them. That is *attitude*. The whole reason you are targeting this job is because of the *hwyl*. Some of those currently in this field may have grown jaded over the years, others may never have thought of it as their ideal job. Not so for you. From day one your enthusiasm will be radiant and your energy levels volcanic. At least on this K2, you'll be top of the tree.

How to Find Out?

How can you find out about job market attractiveness and your prospective K2 rating in a field you may know little about? It's not as difficult as you may think. But it will involve picking up the telephone.

There are two main sources of information available for researching job markets and your potential positioning:

- The Internet and other sources of third-party market research (see Chapter 2).
- Structured interviewing (see Chapter 6).

Compared to the interviewing you did in Chapter 6 concerning your current job, inter-viewing for your target job will have two additional complications:

- You need to interview both customers and providers.
- You may well not know any customers or providers!

It's not as daunting as it may seem. Remember you'll have a storyline with which people can empathize. You're interested in this field of work and would like to find out more about it. You'll find people who'll be delighted to help—not all, but some. The biggest challenge is actually summoning the guts to pick up a phone in the first place and call someone cold.

In summary, here's how (grab a copy of this book's big sister, *Backing U!,* if you'd like more detail):

- Select a representative range of provider and customer interviewees, preferably with some sort of a referee, no matter how obscure, to break the ice. A "warm" interview, even if it's only an acquaintance of a friend of a friend of the family, is always better than a cold call.
- Prepare your storyline, and make it unthreatening and upbeat.
- Prepare a concise questionnaire for providers and a separate one for customers, which will be for guidance purposes only and not to be adhered to rigorously.
- Interview them face-to-face, if possible, via telephone, even email, if not and make sure you squeeze in answers to the most important questions in whatever time is available.
- Thank them and give them some feedback. Leave a good impression—you never know when your paths may cross again.

How Is the Job Looking Now?

You've done your research. You now have a firmer idea on how attractive the market is for your target job or business. Likewise you're clearer on how well placed you'd be in that job and on how satisfying the job would be.

Does this job still look like a winner? Or has the research proved the contrary? Is it time to draw a line under this target job? Rather than embarking on a job hunt in this field, with all that entails—job searches, application letters, follow-up calls, interviews, and all else—should you cut your losses now? And move on to researching the next job on your shortlist, your backup job?

What are your planned earnings in the target job in three years' time? Are these plans consistent (see Chapter 7) with what your research suggests will happen in the market? Are they consistent with your likely lowly K2 rating when you start the job?

What are the risks of you not making that plan? Is there a showstopper risk (see Chapter 8)? What's the balance of risk and opportunity in you switching to this target job?

Don't be disheartened if there seem to be quite a few big risks! What did you expect? You'll be the new guy. It's bound to be risky!

But what is this life if you take no risks? Nothing ventured, nothing gained, as the saying goes.

What's the storyline for backing you in your target job (see Chapter 9)? Would you back U? Or should you move on to researching the backup job?

Would Selina Back Her Little Shop for Horrors?

Selina was excited to find that the clear winner from Chapter 16's screening process was her children's boutique idea, Little Shop for Horrors. She set out enthusiastically with her research, starting with market demand prospects, as per Chapter 2. She soon found good data off the web on U.K. consumer spending on children's clothing, which had grown steadily over the last few years. On the competitive environment, as per Chapter 3, she knew the only direct competitors in Stratford were her current employer, Ellis's, and its rival, Morgan's, both old-style departmental fashion stores. There were a few more distant competitors, including a larger department store, a nationwide chain, and a boutique in the county capital, Warwick, 10 miles away. Some locals would go for occasional shopping expeditions to the regional capital, Birmingham, just 40 miles away. Finally, there was also tough and growing competition from catalog and e-commerce sites.

Selina set about her direct research. She carefully prepared her storyline and divided her questionnaire into those questions she had to have answers to, such as on low volume bargaining with suppliers, and those it would be nice to have, such as on differentiating from the competition, in case she met someone who was prepared to tell all.

She didn't have much luck with the Warwick or Birmingham boutiques. The proprietors were either absent, busy, or wary.

Only one gave her 10 minutes, and that was mainly a moan about current business difficulties, possibly aimed at putting Selina off her quest. Her luck turned when she visited Bath, 85 miles away, and found a boutique proprietor who was proud of having grown a thriving business, felt unthreatened, and even agreed to act as Selina's mentor!

Selina wrote up her research and concluded Chapter 9–style, as follows.

Selina has the skills and drive needed to succeed with a children's boutique in Stratford, but competition may be tough and she needs training in financial management:

- *Market demand prospects*—Demand for children's clothing in Stratford seems set to maintain steady growth, although it is highly seasonal and sensitive to an economic downturn.
- *Competition*—Competition will depend partly on who succeeds Selina at Ellis's, and may get tougher as e-commerce grows in this erstwhile protected retail segment.
- *Selina's K2 rating*—Selina has the fashion purchasing and selling skills needed to succeed, but has little experience in finance, especially cash flow management.
- *Selina's plan*—Selina's plan for Little Shop for Horrors assumes market share gain from Ellis's, but seems reasonably robust and endorsed (unofficially) by a peer; it should enable her to meet her earnings expectations within two years of trading.
- *Risks and opportunities*—The main

risks of Ellis's hiring a children's wear specialist replacement and of Selina struggling with financial management seem surpassed by her determination, enthusiasm, and business capabilities.

Would Selina back herself in this new venture? Oh, yes! Would Chuck Cash? Surely yes, Selina thought. But just to be on the safe side, she should have a firm strategy for how to launch and build this business. That's for the next chapter.

Would Roger Back Himself in Teaching?

Roger is a self-employed IT professional, but the job that emerged as most promising from Chapter 16's screening, namely teaching, implied a return to being an employee. Roger resolved to look into all angles of this dramatic career change.

Roger didn't have Selina's problems of gathering first-hand information. While boutique proprietors can be cagey about talking to a potential competitor, the same tends not to hold true for public sector workers, especially teachers. Roger started by meeting two officials at the Ministry of Education at the provincial government of British Columbia, and they were most helpful. They confirmed that Roger would need to complete a post-graduate certificate in education, which he could do either in one year on a full-time basis, or in two years part-time.

They gave him some contact names

of specialist IT teachers at a half-dozen elementary schools in the area, and soon he was able to meet with three of them.

Two were encouraging, even soothing regarding Roger's concerns over how to deal with unruly pupils, but one was outright discouraging. Clearly her heart was no longer in teaching, so Roger advised her to read this book. But he found out what he needed to know. These were his objective, Chapter 9–style conclusions.

Roger has the subject qualifications, experience, and attitude for a career in a buoyant IT teaching market, but his teaching credentials remain untested:

- *Market demand prospects*—Demand for IT teachers at elementary schools in British Columbia is steadily growing.
- *Competition*—There is a current shortage of IT teachers, filled temporarily by foreigners on contract, which should last until balance is returned in two to three years' time.
- *Roger's K2 rating*—Roger has the appropriate IT qualifications and experience and his attitude seems positive, but he has no teaching experience so it remains unproven that he would thrive in the job.
- *Roger's plan*—Roger's plans to downscale his family spending and live within a teacher's means seem reasonably thought through.
- *Risks and opportunities*—The main risk of teaching proving not to be Roger's métier needs mitigating, but

seems balanced by his evident desire for greater security and meaning from his work.

Roger wonders if this storyline will be convincing enough to gain Chuck's backing. It seems borderline. He had better prepare an entry strategy that addresses the main risk of teaching turning out to be not his thing. That's for Chapter 18.

In Short

Research your target job for satisfaction, market attractiveness, and K2 rating.

Would you back U in that target job?

If not, research the backup job...

18 Shortening the Odds

Don't be afraid to take a big step. You can't cross a chasm in two small jumps.—David Lloyd George

In the last chapter, you found a job or business with *hwyl* where you may well be backable.

Let's pause there for a moment. That's already some achievement! You have a chance at landing a job of your dreams. Or not far off. Isn't that amazing? You're on the verge of setting off on a course that could change your life.

But before you do, there's one further step. From all the research you conducted in the last chapter on your target job, did you find anything you could or should be doing *now, before* you set off in pursuit of this new job?

This is where the tools deployed in Part II of this book may be of help. To what extent can you build on your strengths or work on your weaknesses before you set off, or while you are pursuing your target job?

This chapter won't duplicate what's in Part II, which was written largely for making yourself more backable in your current job. But here's a summary of what you should consider doing to make yourself more backable in your target job.

Envision the capabilities of the ideal provider of your target job. Do some brainstorming, some "out-of-the-box" thinking about how things may evolve in the markets and companies you will be serving in the target job. You could try building scenarios ("What if such-and-such happens?"). What then would be the capabilities of the ideal provider of services under each scenario, and which of those capabilities would be common to all or most of the scenarios? See Chapter 10 for further detail.

Set your sights and identify the K2 gap. The gap between your likely K2 rating in your target job and that of the ideal provider will be wide at present. It should narrow over time, if only by virtue of your growing experience as time goes by, but that may not be sufficient. Where do you want to be in three years' time? Be realistic. You won't make it to the ideal provider within three years. But how close can you get? Should you stretch your sights and make your plans more ambitious? Should you "go for goal" (see Chapter 11)? What then is the shortfall between your expected capabilities after three years and those to which you aspire—the K2 gap?

Select your entry strategy for succeeding in your target job. How are you going to bridge this K2 gap? Chapter 12 discusses the three main generic strategies, termed Stand Out!, easyU! and Sharpen Act! You'll have a much better chance of getting in and succeeding in your target job if you have a sound, coherent entry strategy.

A Stand-Out! or easyU! strategy will typically enable you to get into your target job or business more readily than Sharpen Act! If there is something distinctive and differentiating about you, or if you are offering a quality service at a competitive price, you'll be raising your head above the rest.

The Sharpen Act! strategy, where you work on some evident weaknesses as opposed to building on strengths, is more applicable to surviving, even progressing, in your current job. If one of your known areas of weakness is an important K2 in your target job, you may need to think again. You may not be aiming for the right job.

Having selected your generic entry strategy, what are your strategic alternatives within it? If you're to be an employee, what investment should you make in marketing or training? If you're to be self-employed, what investment is needed not just in those two areas, but also in equipment, premises, staff, and partnering?

You need to decide on your most effective strategic alternative(s) and draw up an action plan.

Have you shortened the odds of getting in and succeeding in your target job with *hwyl?*

Has the balance of risks and opportunities in your target job shifted in your favor?

Are you in better shape to embark on your job hunt?

Shortening Selina's Odds

We left off with Selina looks quite backable in her Little Shop for Horrors venture. But how could she become more so?

Selina kicked off with some targeted brainstorming. She and her friend left kids with husbands and hopped down to London for the weekend. They gorged themselves on "retail therapy" among the Bond Street designer boutiques, went to a show featuring music from Selina's favorite band, Queen, dined and wined alfresco, then retreated to the hotel. There Selina soaked in a long, hot bath, and with the inspiring lyrics "Don't stop me now" still buzzing in her ears, let her mind drift....

In the early hours of a Sunday morning, she came up with three scenarios:

- *Tommied!* Thomas Ellis & Co is bought out, thoroughly modernized, and the children's section transformed into a must-shop destination, run by an experienced, dynamic new manager.
- *Ditto!* Another children's boutique opens in Stratford, competing directly with Little Shop for Horrors.
- *Muddle!* Selina makes a serious mess of inventory and/or cash flow management.

The implications for the ideal children's wear boutique business were as follows:

- *Tommied!* It must be a compelling retail destination from the outset, deterring an Ellis's makeover, emphasizing K2s such as location and décor of premises,

Fit for a King

Suppose, just suppose, a famous son gets fed up with waiting to take over his mom's job. What career can he switch to, now that he's 60? And how can he shorten his odds of success?

He's a man with manifold interests, a passionate espouser of causes dear to his heart. Suppose there are five jobs he rates with the maximum five *hwyl* ticks: architect/town planner, artist, homeopathist, organic farm manager, and environmental campaigner. Of these, suppose it's environmental campaigning on organic farming that emerges in pole position through Chapters 16 and 17.

Time for some brainstorming. He has an array of palaces and mansions from which to choose, but he wisely chooses his latest property, an estate in Wales. From there he can walk up to the bleak, often cold, wet, and windswept mountains of the Brecon Beacons to clear his head. There he conjures up a number of grim scenarios, whereby diseases originating from intensive farming spiral out of control.

He envisages the ideal campaigner, someone experienced not only in organic and alternative farming methods, but who understands and can communicate the science behind modern farming methods. He sets his sights, goes for goal, and aims to fully bridge the K2 gap with a Stand-Out! strategy.

He identifies two areas where he needs to prepare himself for his job switch. First, he needs to raise his understanding of the underlying science from that of interested amateur to semiprofessional. He'll embark on an intensive tutoring program in modern agricultural science.

Second, he's aware that his clipped, rather pon-
derous speaking style may need to be adapted for
motivational speaking. He'd benefit from regular
practice in front of an empathetic audience, so he
resolves to set up a Toastmasters Club (see Chapter
12) at St. James' Palace! He asks me for help (?!).
Armed with these plans, he calls in Chuck Cash. One
of the most sensational job shifts in history. Watch this
space... (NOT!).

clothing range, and marketing.

- *Ditto!* The same, preempting a direct
  competitive startup.
- *Muddle!* The financial management K2
  must be learned or brought in.

Selina wasn't overly troubled by these
findings. She knew retail was tough, but so
was she, and she was determined to go for
goal (see Chapter 11). She resolved to bridge
the K2 gap by adopting an unashamed Stand
Out! strategy, backed up by these initiatives:

- In décor, range, and marketing she
  would invite her new mentor, the
  successful boutique owner in Bath,
  to advise her on a more formal and
  commercial basis, either on a success-
  related, deferred fee basis or by taking
  a slice of the equity
- Selina would enroll for evening
  classes in financial management and
  accounting at Stratford-upon-Avon
  College

Selina was ready to put her plans to Chuck

Cash. He was impressed. Selina seemed to have thought through the main issues facing her new venture. And she had developed a stand-out entry strategy to minimize her risks. All she needed now was some help in refining her rather crude financial forecasts, but that was what Chuck was for.

Subject to tweaking the numbers, Chuck would back her. He'd back the *hwyl*.

Shortening Roger's Odds

Roger's a decent golfer, not a great one—no single-digit handicap—but no rabbit either. For his brainstorming exercise, he treated himself to a solo visit to Furry Creek Golf & Country Club, one of British Columbia's most scenic courses, with panoramic views of mountains and sea. Halfway round the course (while only six over par), he ventured off the beaten track, climbed a hill, pulled out his picnic bag, gazed at the deep blue Pacific and pondered his future in elementary school IT teaching.

Unlike for Selina, Roger didn't see the main issues being around the market. They were around Roger himself and his K2 rating. He developed two scary scenarios:

- *Anarchy!* Roger finds it hard to control his class. He becomes anxious, his control weakens further and a vicious circle ensues.
- *Awkward!* Roger finds it hard to return to being an employee, with performance targets set and monitored by a head teacher possibly younger than him.

Roger didn't see what he could do about the Awkward! scenario. He would just have to learn to live with the reality of being answerable to a younger person, a situation that many career changers have to live with. He would have to swallow that most deadly of the seven sins: pride.

But Furry Creek inspired a stroke of genius around the Anarchy! scenario. By taking a Sharpen Act! strategy to an extreme, he might be able to deploy a Stand Out! His brother-in-law was a lawyer and helped out disadvantaged youngsters now and again at a youth center in a poor neighborhood in downtown Eastside. He had often told Roger of the challenging but fulfilling work done by volunteers at the center. Perhaps Roger could enroll as one such volunteer and conduct weekly classes in IT while studying for his certificate in education. The experience gained in learning how to control classes of underprivileged, potentially unruly teenagers should hold him in good stead for classes of nine-year-olds from mixed socioeconomic backgrounds.

Roger was ready to talk to Chuck again. Chuck liked what he heard—the attitude, the determination, the strategy. Roger was looking backable.

In Short

Envision the ideal provider and identify the K2 gap.

Select your entry strategy to bridge the gap.

Are U now more backable?

19 Now Back the *Hwyl!*

Do, or do not. There is no try.—Yoda

Now it's time to go out and get that job. Or start that business. It's time to back the *hwyl!*

Here are a dozen choice tips along the way.

Find Your Ideal Employer
Tip #1—Don't quit your job until you have the next one lined up!

Employers will look on you more favorably if you have a busy work schedule than if you evidently have time on your hands. When you're working, your energy levels are higher, your time is tighter, and this will come through in the interview. If you're unavoidably "in-between jobs" because you had no choice but to quit or were laid off, you'll need to prepare thoroughly for the interview. You'll have to greatly raise both knowledge and energy levels before stepping into the room.

Tip #2—Don't wait for the employer to come to you. Go to the employer!

Identify the companies you want to work for and approach them directly. You may have already spoken to them in your Chapter 17 research. They may not have a job vacancy available, but one may appear soon. And they could create an additional place just for you. Why? Because of your *hwyl!*

Land the Interview

Tip #3—Wherever possible, start the cover letter with a referral.

Most unsolicited letters enquiring about a job opportunity end up if not in the trash can then with the standard, pro forma rejection letter. Your chances of receiving one of these may well be reduced if you can sneak some sort of a referral into the opening paragraph—even if it's just the name of the person from Marketing who brushed you off!

Tip #4—Customize the cover letter for *that* job in *that* company.

The cover letter is an opportunity to show that you have a sound understanding of the company and why it would be to their benefit to hire someone like you. Each job, each company is special. So too must be each letter.

Tip #5—Tailor your résumé for *that* job in *that* company.

Is there any one element of your experience or qualifications that could be more relevant to that job in that company? If so, this should be highlighted in your résumé.

Tip #6—Chase!

If you hear from the company within two

to three weeks, fine. If not, call them up. Fear not, chase them. Remember, this is a job with *hwyl* you're after.

Perform at the Interview

Tip #7—Dress to impress!

Here's a rule of thumb: Be as well dressed as the best-dressed person in the room.

Companies tend to recruit in their own likeness. Period.

Tip #8—Talk about why the company needs you!

What really impresses the interviewer is when you have a coherent storyline on what *you* could do for *them*. You should bubble with knowledge and ideas on where the company is heading and how you stand ready to play your part in helping them get there.

Tip #9—Sit alert.

You need to be attentive and on the ball. You should be in the classic TV interview pose. Back straight and leaning slightly forward. At around 75 degrees. Then you can perform at your best while seated.

Tip #10—Perform!

It's not just what you say, it's how you say it. Imagine you're on stage. The curtain goes up, the lights come on, and yes, it's show time! Time to perform!

Need some practice? Join Toastmasters (see Chapter 12). The skills you learn there will fully equip you for the interview process.

You'll learn how to communicate better, not just speaking to a roomful of people, but one-to-one. You'll learn how to use your voice, your face, your hands, your body in improving your communicating skills. You'll learn how to work with words. You'll learn how to persuade, inspire, and entertain. You'll learn how to perform.

Follow Up the Interview
Tip #11—Send a note.
You enjoyed the meeting. Write and let the interviewer know, by email, snail mail, or both, as appropriate, soon after the meeting. Tell her that you hope she enjoyed it too and found it useful. Remind her of your contact details. And let her know that if she needs any further information you'd be pleased to let her have it.

Tip # 12—Chase again!
Allow the company three to four weeks. If you haven't heard by then, send a gentle prompt. Ask them if there's been any further progress, or if they've had any further thoughts. Ask them if there's anything further they'd like to discuss with you, or anyone else they feel you should meet. If there's still no reply, call them. Keep chasing until you know the answer, one way or another.

Or...Start Your Own Business!
On the other hand, the target career with *hwyl* that emerged from Chapter 17 may be starting your own business. Like Selina in her children's boutique startup.

The great thing about going solo is that you won't have to do any of the above hustling for interviews and pretending you're someone you're not in the interview. Even better, you won't have to do any crawling to the boss. Ever. You're the boss.

But do think twice. It's not for everybody. It can be hard. You'll find yourself having to do "interviews" again and again, except that they'll be to customers. They're pitches for work. And although you're the boss, you're also the gofer (see Chapter 13).

Remember you'll have one enormous advantage in starting this business. You'll have the *hwyl*. Your competitors may no longer feel it. You'll have an edge.

Now Back the *Hwyl!*

Life is in the living of it.—Leo Tolstoy

You're ready. Don't procrastinate. Take the plunge. A new work life beckons. One with *hwyl*.

You won't work to live. You won't live to work. You'll live.

It's time to back the *hwyl*. It's time to back U.

Good luck. *Pob hwyl.*

You can get it if you really want.—Jimmy Cliff

Conclusion

*You must be the change you wish to see
in the world.*—Mahatma Gandhi

In the introduction to this book, we learned
that roughly half of U.S. and U.K. employees were dissatisfied with their jobs. You may
be, or may have been, one of them.

It may be that you were one of those who
thought things were better elsewhere. But
you found out from Part I that you're better
off staying where you are. You're backable in
your current job or business.

You then learned in Part II some techniques on how to make yourself more backable in your current job. And hopefully more
satisfied, more fulfilled.

On the other hand, you may have
learned from Part I that you're not backable
in your current job or business. This may be
because of issues affecting the market as a
whole, or affecting just your company. It may
be because you don't have the capabilities of
your peers. Or it may be because you don't
enjoy your job. And this shows through in
your attitude.

So you followed the techniques of Part
III and found a target job or business with
hwyl. You found a job where you'd be back-

able. You drew up an entry strategy to make yourself more backable. You're ready to set off, and you've picked up a few practical tips for the journey ahead.

Whether you've chosen to move forward in your current job or business, or move across to one with *hwyl*, I hope you've found some of the techniques in this book useful. I hope you're now more backable.

I hope you'll carry on Backing *U!*

Postscript

Has this book helped you? If you've had a recent job shift, would it have been of help? Please let me know.

I'm working on a follow-up to this book. It's called *You Backed U!* and includes a series of examples of how the techniques of this book have helped people. I'd like to select a dozen or so examples of people who've benefited from Parts I and II. And a similar number who've benefited from Parts I and III.

You Backed U! aims to be inspirational. By the example of others, it hopes to inspire people to claim greater satisfaction from their current jobs, or businesses. Or switch to others where the passion lies.

Please let me know. Email me at vaughan@youbackedu.com.

I won't be able to write up all your stories, only a couple of dozen. You can appear in the book under your own name, with or without a mug shot, or under a pseudonym. It's up to you.

I look forward to hearing how *You Backed U!*

The quality, not the longevity, of one's life is what is important.—Martin Luther King

Appendix A
Glossary

Backing U! – investing in / putting money on / supporting / having faith in U!

Brainstorming – thinking "out of the box", stimulating the right side of the brain, to develop scenarios (see Chapter 10).

Business chunks – segments of your business or job which have distinct services (or products) and customer groups (Chapter 1).

Business plan – where you plan to be in three to five years' time, strategically and financially, and how you're going to get there (Chapter 7)

Chuck Cash – our mythical investor who is thinking of backing U (Introduction).

Competitive intensity – a measure of how tough competition is in a marketplace (Chapter 3).

Customer needs – what customers need from their service providers (Chapter 4).

Demand drivers – factors which influence market demand (Chapter 2)

easy U! – a generic strategy focused on being a low cost provider (Chapter 12).

Going for goal – stretching your sights and aiming for the ideal provider (Chapter 11).

Ideal provider – the provider who rates most highly against each Key Kapability (Chapter 10).

Hwyl – a Celtic concept of passion, fervor, spirit (Part III).

Key Kapabilities ("K2s") – what service providers need to have or do to succeed in their job or business (Chapter 5).

K2 rating – a measure of competitive position, of how you stack up compared to your competitors (Chapter 6).

Market demand – the aggregate will of consumers in your marketplace to purchase the services provided or products produced (Chapter 2).

Must-have K2s – those essential K2s in a marketplace without which a service provider cannot begin to compete (Chapter 6).

Risk and opportunity – it is the balance of risks and opportunities, assessed by likelihood of happening and impact if they did, which will determine Chuck Cash's backing decision (Chapter 8).

Service provider – a self-employed businessperson engaged in providing a service for customers, or an employee for his/her managers or "customers" (Chapter 1).

Sharpen Act! – a generic strategy focused on improving competitiveness, including working on weaknesses (Chapter 12).

Stand Out! – a generic strategy focused on differentiating through your strengths (Chapter 12).

Strategy – how you deploy your resources to gain a sustainable competitive advantage over the competition (Chapter 12).

U – you, a backable entity, whether an employee or self-employed.

UCo – your company, whether self-employed or with employees engaged (Chapter 13).

Appendix B
Recommended Reading

There are many books on career development and change. Here are a dozen of the best.

Richard Nelson Bolles, *What Color Is Your Parachute? 2009: A Practical Manual for Job-Hunters and Career-Changers,* Ten Speed Press, 2008

William Bridges, *Creating You & Co,* Perseus Books, 1997

Po Bronson, *What Should I Do with My Life?: The True Story of People Who Answered the Ultimate Question,* Ballantine, 2005

Marcus Buckingham & Donald O. Clifton, *Now, Discover Your Strengths,* Free Press, 2001

Vaughan Evans, *Backing U! A Business-Oriented Guide to Backing Your Passion and Achieving Career Success,* Business & Careers Press, 2009

Barrie Hopson and Mike Scally, *Build You Own Rainbow: A Workbook for Career and Life Management,* Management Books 2000, 2004

Julie Jansen, *I Don't Know What I Want, but I Know It's Not This,* Piatkus, 2003

John Lees, *How to Get a Job You'll Love, 2009/2010 Edition: A Practical Guide to Unlocking Your Talents and Finding Your Ideal Career,* McGraw-Hill Professional, 2008

Carol L. McClelland, *Your Dream Career for Dummies,* For Dummies, 2005

Daniel Porot, *The PIE Method for Career Success: A Unique Way to Find Your Ideal Job,* JIST Works, 1995

Barbara Sher, *I Could Do Anything if I Only Knew What It Was: How to Discover What You Really Want and How to Get It,* Dell, 1995

Nick Williams, *The Work We Were Born to Do: Find the Work You Love, Love the Work You Do,* Element Books, 2000

About the Author

VAUGHAN EVANS is well placed to guide you on backing U! For the last thirty five years, he has advised clients on whether they should invest in businesses, large and small. He found that the tools he developed work just as well on the individual. An economist, strategy consultant, corporate financier, small businessman, politician, and speaker, he has reinvented himself on numerous occasions, honing his *Backing U!* tools in the process. He has worked at investment bankers Bankers Trust and management consultants Arthur D. Little. An economics graduate of Cambridge University and an Alfred P. Sloan fellow with distinction of London Business School, he spent the first dozen years of his career living in exotic lands like the West Indies, Fiji, and Thailand. He hails from West Wales, no less lovely a land, and a cradle of *hwyl*.

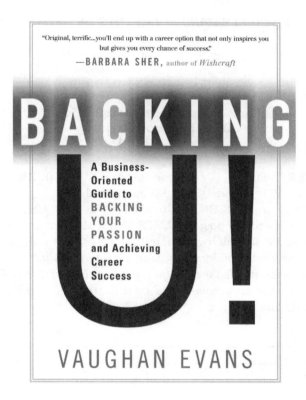

Give the Gift of

Backing U! LITE

to Your Friends and Colleagues

CHECK YOUR LEADING BOOKSTORE OR ORDER HERE

Online: **www.AtlasBooks.com**
Toll-free telephone (24/7): **800-247-6553**;
or fax: **419-281-0200**

Mail: **Atlas Books Distribution**
30 Amberwood Parkway
Ashland, OH 44805

☐ **YES**, I want _____ copies of *Backing U! LITE* (ISBN 978-0-9561391-1-5) at US$14.95 each, and/or _____ copies of *Backing U!* (ISBN 978-0-9561391-0-8) at US$24.95 each, plus $5.50 postage (USPS Media Mail) for one book and $1.00 for each additional book. *(Please ask about postage costs for larger, faster, or international orders. Ohio residents please add appropriate sales tax. Canadian orders must be accompanied by a postal money order in U.S. dollars.)*

Name_____

Address_____

Phone_____

E-mail_____

☐   My check or money order for $_____ is enclosed.

    Or please charge my credit card:
☐ Visa ☐ MasterCard ☐ Discover ☐ American Express

Card #_____ Expiry date_____

Signature_____

Thank you for your order!